One Breath at a Time

One Breath at a Time

The Autobiography of an Artist

DAVID GERBSTADT

Printed by Create Space

©2011 by David Gerbstadt

All rights reserved. No part of this book may be reproduced in any form or by electronic or mechanical means. Including information storage and retrieval systems, without permission in writing from the author, except by a reviewer who may quote brief passages in a review.

Artwork on page: 63, 79, 162 by David Gerbstadt
Photos as noted by Dr. Christine Gerbstadt

Cover design by: David Gerbstadt

Photograph on cover and on page 221
By: Tony & Elaine Babcock of
Visual Perceptions
www.visualperceptions.biz

Some names have been changed or edited to protect privacy.

ISBN- 978-0-9849606-0-6

Visit David Gerbstadt on face book
www.gerbstadt.net

For all those who helped me heal
and for all those who have been there…

Contents

ACKNOWLEDGMENTS	10
FORWARD BY THE AUTHOR	13
YOU CAN'T STOP GERBSTADT	16
MY FIRST LOVE	19
TRACTOR TRAILER TRUCK VS. BICYCLE RIDER	25
THE JOURNAL BY DR. CHRISTINE GERBSTADT LAURA DICK	30
DAVID'S JOURNAL	59
OUT OF THE DANGER ZONE	118
WHEN AN ARTIST DIES	119
COMING BACK TO LIFE	120
WHAT SAVED ME?	121
MY SISTER	131
GOING HOME	151
HOME	155
WHY DOES THE WORLD NEED THIS BOOK?	156
PART 2	157

THE ACT OF DRAWING!	159
THE BUDDY SYSTEM - MENTOR/GOOD FRIEND	163
ACTION	164
SWEEP AND STARE AT THE WALL	167
BUMPS IN THE ROAD	168
SITTING AND WATCHING THE WORLD GO BY	169
CINCH BY THE INCH	170
LAUGH AND BE SILLY	171
BEAMED DOWN	173
DO WHAT YOU LOVE LOVE WHAT YOU DO	174
SNACK TIME	175
MUFFIN WITH FRIEND	176
SEEING OUT THE WINDOW	177
KILL THEM WITH KINDNESS	179
LIFE WITHOUT MUSIC IS A MISTAKE	180
THIS IS NOT A BRAIN TUMOR	181
LOSING SIGHT	182

RULES FOR PLAY	184
NEVER SAY CAN'T	185
KEEP ON FUNKING ON	186
CHRISTINE	187
LOVED ONES DYING	188
FEEL WHAT YOU FEEL	189
FIND SOMEONE YOU TRUST AND TELL YOUR FEELINGS TO THEM	190
JOURNAL OR WRITE SOMETHING	191
GIVE YOURSELF A BREAK	192
PLAY	193
LAUGH	194
CONSCIOUS STATE OF MIND	195
YOUR STORY	196
DO NOT BE AFRAID TO BE WRONG	197
DO IT ANYHOW	198
SPIRITS ARE ALL AROUND	200
SPIRIT HOUSES	201
RETURNING TO THE ART	203

ONE YEAR LATER	204
SURVIVING AMONG THE LIVING	209
NOEL	220
ABOUT THE AUTHOR	222

ACKNOWLEDGMENTS

This book wouldn't have been written without the help of many people.

My dear friend Robert, who told me what Jasper Johns said about making art, "Do something, do something to that, and then do something to that." Robert told me to "just start writing and add something each day. You can stare at the page if you have nothing to say. Just make the effort to write this book." Robert says every few phone calls, "You can't stop Gerbstadt!" Several calls to Robert would consist of me crying uncontrollably. He would kindly scream at me, "YOU GOT RUN OVER BY A SEMI TRUCK! YOU'RE ALLOWED TO CRY!" He would remind me on a regular basis, "You know, Dave, it was not long ago you had a vent tube shoved down your throat!" Robert continues to be a wonderful friend who understands.

So many people were at the right place at the right time, otherwise I would not be here writing this book and sharing my experience, strength, and hope.

Special thanks to all the guys at Sarasota, Florida Station #1 and Jr. Stephens, who gave me CPR and brought me back to life the first time in the ambulance. Thanks also go to the unknown off-duty EMT at the scene, who I am told called in the chopper. And thank you to the helicopter pilot, who flew me to Bay Front Hospital.

My thanks go to all the hospital staff, from the beautiful woman who cleaned my room everyday to the countless nurses and doctors who cared for me.

Thanks to Gail for sending Samuel the bear, who I slept, ate, and went to therapy with.

Thank to Katherine Cotter as my editor.

Thank you to the woman who at 5:00 A.M. came into my hospital room and drew blood for a test. She looked into my eyes after reading my chart. "You have a story to tell and you need to tell it," she said repeatedly to me. I do not know her name. I only saw her once, but she planted the seed for me to write this book.

I have to thank my dear longtime friend Ruth for the many late night phone calls. She is a nurse and understood the importance of this book from the start.

Thanks to the many friends who were there for me throughout this journey. You helped more than you will ever know, even when you had no idea what to do or say. A simple hug was all I needed.

I have to thank myself. This may be a selfish act. I had to overcome my dyslexia to complete this book. I am glad I worked to achieve my goal. Throughout the writing of this book I doubted myself. Then I thought to myself, just write and see where it leads; just do the writing, and it will all work out the way it is supposed to. I had to get my thoughts and trauma out. Who cares what others think or say about it? Write and write and write! Once I made the conscious decision to write this book, the words just flowed.

The cost of the book was a way, perhaps, to take myself out of low-paying jobs and do what I wanted to do—create and make a living as an artist!

I owe a lot to so many people who sent me cards, letters, books, CDs, tapes, and so on. I have no idea as to who sent a lot of my mail. I was on many prayer lists. Scores of people called me who had never called me before. I had several visitors in the hospital who had traveled several hundred miles to see me.

Staff at the hospital went out of their way to just visit me: Tina from the children's hospital, who brought ice cream, and Nurse Gail from the operating room came by several times. Heather, who worked in respiratory therapy, followed me throughout my stay just to say hello. The cleaning woman in ICU was also a blessing. I will never forget her coming to my bedside just to check on me. There were countless doctors and nurses who just wanted to say hello to someone who never gave up!

More thanks go to my friend Tony, who wrote to me while I was in the hospital to tell me about his time as a sniper for the military. He saw my type of accident several times, and all the victims died. He was thrilled to hear I made it. What he described I could relate to as a trauma victim. We both talk about our experience, strength, and hope. Life is easier when there is someone who has been there and empathizes with what you speak of. Tony and I speak each other's language.

For Pea.

For Noel.

Tony Babcock and Eliane Babcock

There are countless others who simply listened to me recount my story, the gist of which is never give up.

FORWARD BY THE AUTHOR

"Got a problem? Do what you can, with what you have, where you are."
—Theodore Roosevelt

As an artist, I have learned that just creating my art and living my life one day at a time has encouraged people to ask for my help, advice, guidance, and my thoughts. Fellow artists and people along my journey have told me they are inspired by and look up to me as well as honor and respect my dedication to my art. I have received phone calls and emails from friends and strangers alike in the middle of the night, telling me how my life and art makes their own lives better and how much it means to them. This, in turn, pours more light into my world, which might not always be so colorful and happy. When anyone asked for help, I was there to do what I could with what I knew at the time.

It took many weeks of musing and concentration to articulate the language I wanted to speak in order to tell my story. Some may not understand my meaning, but hopefully most will.

One afternoon, I was lying on a mat in physical therapy, and the therapist said, "You ever consider writing a book?"

I said, "Yes I have. Do you think I should?"

She looked at me and said, "Yes I think you should!"

Several people in the hospital also told me to tell my story. These workers have seen death, birth, and healing. A listener's eyes would open when I told my tale.

So I set it all down here in order to share my experience, strength, and hope. Perhaps it may help someone else. Maybe it will help you.

One Breath at a Time

YOU CAN'T STOP GERBSTADT!

My good friend often says, "You can't stop Gerbstadt! He will make art out of anything!" That is my philosophy of using what I have where I am to just make art, and I make no excuses to continue with such a philosophy—one which is further strengthened by the words of Winston Churchill:

> "Never give in, never give in, never, never, never, never—in nothing, great or small, large or petty—never give in except to convictions of honor and good sense. Never yield to force. Never yield to the apparently overwhelming might of the enemy."

What started as a one-week Christmas holiday stay with my sister in Sarasota, Florida turned into three and half months of unexpected events and personal challenges. I had managed to leave work during the busy season and fly down to the sun and sand. Arriving the Sunday before Christmas was a wonderful feeling.

My mom died the year before from multiple myeloma, and we all miss her terribly. She fought two years with cancer and died just short of fifty years of marriage. She had a glorious and beautiful life. At age fifty, she just started running, and before long she was collecting medals and trophies. She inspired countless people in the community with her running triathlons, marathons, and her visits to the senior games.

So, it was on a day when the warm sun and proximity to the beach tempted me to take advantage of my sister's bicycle. It beckoned me from the garage, so I rode often, always making sure to wear a helmet. I loved riding into town for lunch, peddling to the beach, or to an A.A. meeting.

This ride was the gateway into a new world. The universe was about to reveal all its glory and power to me in one beautiful moment, but it was up to me to take the first steps before anything could or would be discovered.

I think often of the first biography I ever wrote. I was a schoolboy in 6th grade, and my subject was Winston Churchill. He forever changed my life. I refer to the events in his life that made men into noble leaders when the world was in dire need of leadership. As a schoolboy, Winston knew that the British Empire would be in great peril and that it was his destiny to save the Empire! He was right! Germany began building an army and navy as it geared up for war. Later, as an adult, Winston spoke in Parliament about Germany and what he thought the Empire should do. Some of his colleagues scoffed at him. After many speeches and much persistence, people slowly took heed to what Winston had to say, and soon the world was at war once again! Winston then became Prime Minister of England.

Winston said, "Painting keeps the black dog at bay," and he also said, "Perhaps in my second life I would become a good painter."

As an artist myself, I just create the art, and, in doing so, I am truly free, knowing I can never do it wrong but can always do it better… I identify with and have seen the black dog of which Winston spoke. The black dog is depression, and painting has kept the black dog at bay for me as well.

People travel the world to see great marvels and eat different foods, and they buy things to remind them of these moments. My experience had me cross the desert. The gods, spirits, and angels spoke to me, and I spoke to them. I was calm and relaxed because panic would make my heart pump faster and give me even less time to live.

My life did not 'flash' before my eyes, and neither were there opening credits to what I did see.

In the world of the living, my heart stopped three times.

When I finally woke, the surgeons were baffled and told me, "You should be dead." They told me this repeatedly, and they left the room shaking their heads as to why I was NOT dead! They had seen the 'numbers' and all of this before. Death was usually the end result.

Not this time!

The sun and wind spoke to me that day, and I spoke back to them.

Only after I was put into the ambulance and gave the paramedics my name did I start to pray. Then I passed from the world of the known living to where silence and pure light filled my senses.

It was beautiful.

This is my story…

MY FIRST LOVE

We all have a first love. Mine is still with me. My love knew me and waited patiently till we met.

As a senior in high school, I fought tooth and nail to pass and fill out applications to colleges. The struggle through school made my future quite clear to me—getting into college would be nearly impossible!

But as long as we know where we stand and what we have to work with, we should never give up!

With my father's help, we attacked the enrollment process as a general would conquer and get what he is after. You have to move a ton of earth to get gold, and the first few colleges were our ton of earth. Some colleges simply looked at the numbers and said no. At a few colleges, we found people literally occupying space at the admission department.

Then came our seventh battle. With the valuable knowledge and language we had previously gained, we entered the office. A young man held all the papers needed for admission, and I knew we had to work harder! We sized him up and started looking for a spot to wedge ourselves in. But the guy was not budging.

I proceeded to tell him of my learning disability, as well as the work I had done outside of school.

He said, "I read here you were awarded Eagle Scout."

"Yes, I am," I said proudly. I saw my spot opening, and I started to wedge my way in. "I work harder than average students to do what comes natural them. I just need more help in learning the material. I can do the work!"

The guy caved.

I was wedging myself in deep then! It was time to go for the throat. "I want into your college. I know the numbers do not warrant an entry, but my other activities have merit."

The man looked at me and then at the papers before leaning in to say, "I am going to take a chance with you and enroll you under one condition: you have to come back in two weeks and start the six-week Pace Program with 120 other students. Do not tell anyone I did this for you. Technically, you are not able to come here. I will also connect you with Dr. Plank. He will help you with your learning disability."

We left his office knowing then more than ever: never give up!

I graduated from high school, and, two weeks later, while seniors were heading for the beach to work or party, I was off to college. I met with Dr. Plank, who had his Doctorate in Education and was severely learning disabled himself. I can tell you that several boxes of tissues were used to dry my tears in his office.

He said, "You can do this. You just have to learn how to work the system."

So I dried my tears, learned all I could over the next six weeks, and tried to pass the courses I had been assigned.

Colleges love paper work, stamps, and signatures. But having a stamp, I found, was just an illusion of power, so I decided to treat college as a game and have as much fun as I did in scouting. In scouting, there are many skills to learn, and they all build upon each other. Once you mastered a skill, you received a signature in your book, and you ADVANCED! Ha!

Once, I found out I had to go to a certain building to get a stamp in one office, go upstairs to another office to get signed, and go back down again to file the form. It was just like scouting! I studied the campus, learned every building and their purposes, and gained valuable information. But when the six weeks neared their end, every student was excited except for me. One day, we were all in our seats, waiting for class to begin.

Everyone was saying, "Only five more days!"

I spoke up and said, "Yes, and four more years!" No one got it and just kept talking.

The professors had a dinner to honor the students that did well over the six weeks, but I did not even come close to receiving an award.

One female professor went to the podium. She said, "I overheard students were counting down the days before they could leave. They said we have only five more days! One student said bluntly, "yes we have five more days and four more years!"

I was shocked! A professor quoted me! To hell with winning a piece of paper—my words were used in a speech by a professor! And she went on to say that, yes, we did have four more years.

Well, out of the 120 students who started the Pace Program with me, only four were allowed admission to the college. And I was one of the four—all because someone took a chance on me!

My first full semester started in the fall of 1987. I took three classes for twelve credits: Wood I, thinking I wanted to be an Industrial Arts major; Stage Craft, to give me a taste of what it might be like as a Communications major; and, just for the hell of it, a studio arts fundamentals course. In the book it read, "Studio Fun." HA! Perfect!

I dreaded the wood course. It was too technical and boring. The stage craft class was also boring, and I decided not to pursue it.

The fundamental studio arts class, though, opened my eyes to creating art. Yes, I had a couple art classes in high school and found them to be a chore because I was not encouraged and had no stimulation or motivation. But what I found in pursuing art in college was not work but the blossoming of a passion and the beginning of a love affair.

I remember opening up my mind but not listening to the professor beyond his demonstrations. I would build sculptures using M&M candies. During one class, I remember, I was off in the corner, building something as usual. The professor had a few students huddled around, baffled at the assignment. Frustrated after trying to explain the assignment so many times, he pointed to me and said, "Look! See David? He is off in the deep end just doing it!"

Hearing my name, I raised my head, turned, and said, "What?!"

"Nothing, David. It is a complement. You're doing great. Go back to work!"

So, I did, and I stepped back to look at the dinosaur head I had sculpted. I had put on a big square made to look like a die. The whole thing was on wheels so it could be pulled.

The professor came over and said, "Cool! Hmm… needs a tail though."

"Your right," I said.

"Put a tail on it in a couple minutes, and if it holds for thirty seconds you get an A for the piece."

"You're on!" I said. I grabbed some pipe cleaners, whipped up a tail, and slapped it onto my sculpture! It stayed for more than thirty seconds, and I did get an A!

I love making ART!

When the semester began to wind down, the professor wanted to speak to me. I sat down, and he said, "You're good. You should take more art classes and declare art as your major."

I looked at him and thought of how much fun I had and would have. "Yes, I will do it," I said.

The next semester was full of art classes that worked my brain in a whole new way, and I loved it!

One day, in the hallway of the art building before class, I made a vow to myself aloud. I said, "For richer or poorer, in sickness or in health, I will make art." I was in love with art and very serious about being an artist. After I did this, creating art became second nature.

I had found my first love.

Thank goodness I went to high adventure camp at Philmont Scout Ranch in Cimarron, New Mexico and to the National Jamboree, where I learned survival skills. After that, talking to professors was easy!

They all said at the beginning of their courses, "If you have a problem come see me!"

I wrote their building and office numbers down. So later, when students in my class were freaking out and worried about going to our professor, I was already in the office. I took their tests while taking my time, and I 'worked' the system.

But, yes, I did screw up! I am human after all!

I quickly found drinking, and I paid the price for it.

It took me five and half years to finish college. Along the way, I failed all my required sciences and had to retake them. I held off till my last semester for that. By that time, though, I learned what to take and what not to take.

Dr. Plank was a huge help for two years. Then one day he said, "I cannot help you anymore. They are making changes here in my department."

So I was cut loose, and I waded into deep waters that threatened to drown me. I sunk a bit—I cannot lie to you—and the drinking grew worse. I fell behind, but I still managed to keep afloat and do what I had to do. I did not cheat. I simply worked their system and never gave up!

When I finished college, I was burnt out. I continued another year deep into my addiction to alcohol and drifting more to drug use before I finally hit bottom. There is no reason to get into or dwell on the war stories of my using. Needless to say, I had started drinking and drugging for self-confidence, social acceptance, and escape. But at the end of my addiction, I was not confident at all but instead a fearful social pariah imprisoned by alcohol and drugs.

One day, I was in a bar during the afternoon, drinking for free for as long as I wanted. Slowly, I looked around the bar, thinking that moment was as good as my life was ever going to be.

My life was beyond unmanageable at that point, and I needed help. Admitting I had a problem and that I needed help got me sober. Since I chose a sober life, I have not had a single drink or drug.

TRACTOR TRAILER TRUCK VS. BICYCLE RIDER

On the morning of December 28, 2007, I borrowed my sister's bicycle and rode into town. At about 11 a.m., I rode back to her house for lunch. No one was home, though, and the house was locked. Without a key, I waited a while for someone to come home.

Looking back, I tell myself not to think, "What if?" What if I had a key? What if I had waited a few more minutes?

I was on my own. So I left towards town to get some lunch and go to an A.A. meeting.

Just a few minutes into my ride, Peter passed me towing his boat back to the house. We waved at each other. That image is one of the last happy moments of my old life. I felt free with the air and warm sunshine. I wore a shirt my brother had given me and my favorite short pants.

The next few minutes of my memory are just of the bumpy ride as I bicycled over the pavement.

The exact moment of the accident is not clear, and everyone on the corner has a different story of how it happened.

Before I knew it, I was on the pavement, and a tractor trailer truck tire was rolling right over my left leg, very close to my pelvis. The crunching of my bone and flesh was muffled as I screamed, "OW!" For just an instant, a flash of white shot through the air and calmed me.

The next instant, my head tilted backwards so I could see I was in the path of the moving rear wheels! In shock and with a broken femur, I managed to drag my body onto the sidewalk. Not feeling any pain, I had no knowledge of just how serious the situation was.

I lay there for a moment, stunned by what just happened. Turning my head, I noticed a huge pool of blood. By touching my head and looking at my hand, I learned it was not coming from my head. So I glanced around to see where the blood was coming from. On my shorts, I saw a circle about seven inches across—maybe more—and the entire pool of blood was the size of my kitchen table. Being an Eagle Scout and trained in first aid, I just reacted and somehow rammed my left hand into the wound.

This simple act alone saved my life.

A few minutes later, the EMTs reached me. With only my sense of hearing remaining, I heard one EMT say, "He is a fucking mess!"

The other EMT said, "Yeah he is! Look, he's holding his wound!"

They had found me without any blood flow and very close to death. Still, they proceeded with their job and never gave up on me!

Then I could feel my bowels empty. The EMTs set to work on me. I could feel them cut off my shirt and short pants with scissors, and I felt movement when they placed the neck brace on before I was moved to the back board.

Another EMT said, "WE HAVE TO DO THIS NOW!"

They got me on the stretcher and rolled me into the ambulance. The oxygen-enriched environment gave me enough of a boost that I could focus on the ceiling of the ambulance and see the EMTs' fire helmets with the number 1 written on them.

The EMT named Jr. was at my head, asking my name.

I spelled my name as loud as I could, and I repeated it.

Turning back to the other EMTs, Jr. said, "I don't know what he is saying. He is just muttering!"

I then began saying the serenity prayer out loud over and over. Perhaps after the second time through, though, everything went white.

No words or expression can properly relate what I saw or experienced. For those who would like some sort of idea as to what I experienced, I can only say that a deep sense of peace and warm love let me know everything would be okay in the end.

Nine hours later, my eyes opened. Some of my ribs were broken and cracked from Jr. performing CPR on me.

Not long after that day when Jr. performed CPR, my sister Christine renewed her CPR training with a class. She told the class that CPR saved her brother's life. The class was composed of only medical workers, and several of the doctors and nurses from other hospitals had heard of my accident.

Both my lungs were collapsed and down to twenty percent production. A vent tube went down my throat to help me breathe, a half-inch tube on each side of me went into my lungs to remove blood that went into bags, and a feeding tube went into my left nostril. The neck brace was still on. A blood pressure cuff on my eggplanted-colored left bicep would go off every fifteen minutes and sent tears to my eyes from the pain. The same eggplant color went up my shoulder and across my entire back. Both legs, from the groin down to my ankles, were packed in thick gauze. More clear tubes ran off of me, taking blood to bags.

My femur was broken and had severed my femoral artery. The surgeon put a titanium rod up through my knee due to the amount of damage to my thigh. A Gortex Graft was put in to repair the artery. I nicknamed my scar "the road map" since it looked like one, with all its long intersecting sections, including thirty-three staples and countless stitches.

My hands were tied to the bed because I was trying to pull out my tubes. I could see and hear everything just fine. Being conscious was by far the worst part of the ordeal. With every breath I took, each injury screamed with pain. In my condition, though, they could not sedate me. I wish they could have.

I wished a lot of things.... The sights, sounds, and feelings will always be forever in my memory. I came back three times from death to survive among the living.

The day of the accident, the small pink card with phone numbers and emergency contact information was found in my wallet. A call was made to my sister, who I had been staying with during the Christmas holiday.

"Hello, is this Christine Gerbstadt?"

"No, this is Peter. Who is calling? Christine will be home soon."

"Oh...are you a family member of David Gerbstadt?"

"No," Peter said.

"Well, I cannot speak to anyone but family members. All I can tell you is that David Gerbstadt is in the ICU of Bay Front Hospital in St. Petersburg, Florida. Come as soon as you can. It is not clear if he will make it through the night."

Peter hung up the phone, and Christine came home a few minutes later. He relayed the phone message, and she then placed the call to my dad and other sister, who were staying in Boca Raton, Florida, and to my brother John, who lives in Maryland.

Christine then grabbed a few things and sped to Bay Front Hospital, crying and saying aloud, "Just be alive when I get there, and I can deal with whatever happens after that." The one-hour drive from her house to the hospital seemed to take forever.

Christine got to my bedside at about nine in the evening, almost nine hours after the accident. She leaned over my bed, looking past all the tubes and wires to see that I was barely hanging on. When she saw me, she just kept saying, "You've been through the worst. It's going to be a long haul, but it's going to be okay."

Through the slits of my eyes, I could see my sister. I knew all that had happened. I had seen, heard, and felt it all....

At one in the morning, my dad and other sister Laura walked into the room. By that time, I was on morphine for the pain, and I hardly even remember them being there.

I spent the next ten days among the dying, with alarms blaring and tubes running in and out of my bloated body. The nights were by far the most horrific between the hours of midnight and six in the morning, when most of the trauma accidents came in. Many of the motorcycle casualties that came into the ICU did not make it through the night. Screams meant the person had life. No screaming, and I knew the person had died.

THE JOURNAL
BY DR. CHRISTINE GERBSTADT AND LAURA DICK

The following is a journal written by my sisters about my stay in the intensive care unit. I was given this journal ten months after the accident. After reading a couple entries, I learned that my condition had been far more serious than I remember now. For a while, I tried to read and transcribe their journal into this book. I could not. The experience was far too emotional for me. Although I could have someone else type the entries for me, somehow it just did not seem like the right thing to do. Then, one morning, I woke up with the answer. I scanned each page of the journal and included the copies in this book. This way, my sisters' feelings could be properly captured in their own handwriting. To this day, I have not read their journal, and I may never in the future. I don't have to…. I lived it.

On December 28, 2007, at approximately noon, I died in an ambulance on the way to a waiting helicopter. I had just been run over by a tractor trailer truck while riding on my bicycle. Over the next few hours, my heart stopped three times. This is my story.

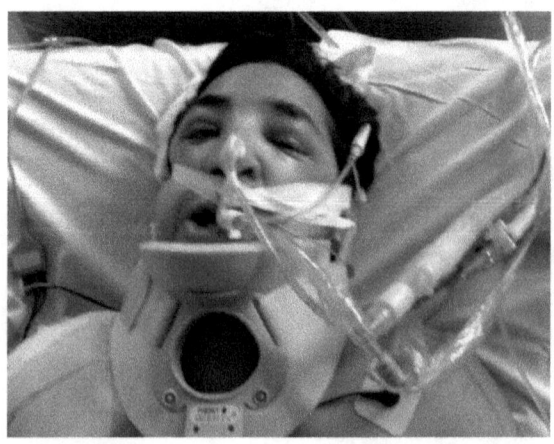

Photo by Dr. Christine Gerbstadt - Waking up

Davids big Nasty Adventure

Friday

12-28   David left Christi's house in Sarasota for a bike ride. He called Fred looking for a place to have lunch.

12:55   At 12:55 at the intersection of 301 & Rt. 17 a semi truck making a left turn collided with his bike causing a tragic accident. The David communicated to Christi on saturday that he saw his leg go under the truck wheel. His femur was broken & ruptured his femoral artery. The EMT relayed to David that he saved his own life by plugging the artery with his hand. EMT arrived in moments & summoned life flight which transported him to Bayside Medical Center in St. Petersburg. At

1:30   1:30pm he was in emergency surgery to repair the damage. ICU nurses stated that he was code blue 3x & had CPR during flight, surgery, and in the ICU. He lost volumes of blood & recieved "dozens" of units. The 4½ hr. surgery repaired the femoral artery with a gortex graft; inserted a rod into his femor, and tubed both his collapsed lungs. They scanned his belly through an incision & found good kidneys, a bruised liver and damage to his spleen.

6:30P Call from Sarasota police to Christine. David had her number in his wallet under emergency contacts.

7:30P Call to Fred. The only information we get is that David was in a seriou accident.

8:15P Dad, Ann & Laura Drive to St. Pete where Christi & Peter are waiting and we arrive @ 12:30 AM.

12:30 AM David is resting in ICU. Lucid, Swollen from all the liquids, communicating by blinking his eyes & squeezing hands. We are all relieved that there was no trauma to his head. He is emotional and we all go to the Hilton to rest.

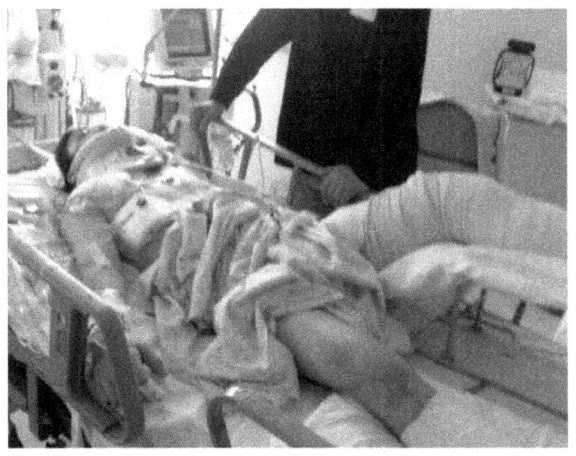

Photo by Dr. Christine Gerbstadt

SAT 12.29

5:00 AM: Laura can't sleep & Christi suggests a visit because hours are restricted from 6:30 - 8:30 AM & PM. We have a nice visit and he is lucid and we try not to excite him. His blood pressure is low so he is not heavily sedated but his heart rate is about 120-145. He is frantically motioning for a drink but of course cannot because he is on a ventilator. We apply vaseline to his lips & go to the hotel.

6:00 AM HILTON: The fire alarm is tripped so we wait in the lobby while sleepy guests evacuate & firemen arrive. False alarm.

10:30 AM - Back in ICU David is doing better. The nurse on duty is Linda and is pleased with his vitals. BP is still low but his lungs are draining well. The left one has more fluid but not alarming.

11:00 David conveys to Christi that

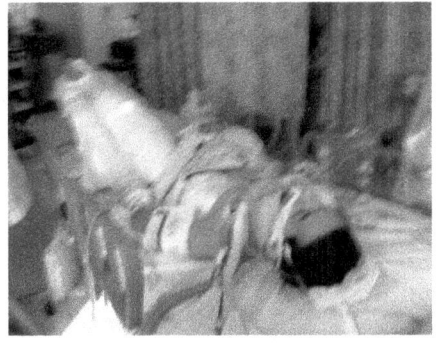

Photo by Dr. Christine Gerbstadt

"he saw the light". His concern is for his students in his "beadolgy" class that they get the information he needs to cancel. He also expresses his wishes to thank the EMT's by creating some art for them. We tell him to use this resting time to create and when he is emotional and begins to cry we tell him to go to his "special place". Laura's is walking in the woods with dogs. He also tells Christi that all his bills are paid for January on line & he banks with Wachovia. Way to go Dave!!

11:43A Trauma surgeon putting in IVC filter & cup line in cordis.

We are asked to leave during procedures

noon: Everyone agrees Fred needs a Niu Niu Sarasota fix so we drive to Sarasota. Christi & Laura do the marketing & it is nice to get a bite to eat & spread out. Alex shows us his toys & plays happily. Peter hits the bed & Christi & Ann get busy preparing lasagna for dinner. She is still ready to take care of the 8 people who are there & life goes on...

2:30 P Laura is back at the hospital & with a letter board gets chastised for hitting the rail because it moves the bed. Unfortunatly, the portable

3:30 P Xray is rolled in and the technician says he is going to be moving more than the rail. No family allowed. They will get chest Xrays.

David's heart rate is about 105 — lower than the morning & his BP has risen slightly, all good signs. 99/53 The drainage from his lungs is stimulated because they turned him. Status Quo. Good. Pam introduced herself in Sarasota as Christi's neighbor. Her husband owns the truck & knows the driver involved in the accident. An odd twist of fate.

4:30 P Still waiting outside. The nurse said it was taking awhile.

4:45 P A lullaby just came over the PA. What a pleasant reminder of birth. Someone has welcomed a new baby! I am overcome with joy.

5:00 P — David looks good. His nurse is watching the swelling in his leg to see if they need to relieve the pressure. He can wiggle his toes & needs to keep moving them. The left leg is not able to dorsiflex due to the injury. We worked on the letter board; his collar was digging into the back of the neck but because there is not a doctor here it can't be removed. Slight adjustment relieved the pressure. David said his friend taught him how to deal with pain; it won't last. Good advice. He needs more xrays but didn't complain about them. His urine output is voluminous. David signed that he doesn't have a spare pair of glasses when asked. His doctor is across from the Wayne library and his boss may know the name.

Linda is nice. We showed her a "before" picture from Alaska. David's temp spiked to 102° earlier but is at 99.9° now. I suggested David rest up for John's visit and said goodbye around 6:00

9:00 PM : Arrived with John after fetching him from the Tampa airport. David's first letter board message was to tell me he napped! Wow! He remembered our conversation & tried to be compliant. That's amazing. He said it wasn't completly restful. Dad arrived so I swapped out & chatted with Ann and realised bed was over due! She has been a trooper blending with our wierd family, can't be easy but she is a gentle soul & does it effortlessly with grace. The new nurse ? promised to bath him tonight & was busy getting 2 units of blood for Dave. His heartrate was about 115 and temp 99.2°. He was sallow but freshly powdered and that looked comfy & refreshing. His lips were moistened.

→ I forgot to tell him Christi went by the fire house & thanked them & got the name of his EMS that saved him. We plan to send them some steaks.

I said goodnight & returned to the hotel. No-one cared when & followed the Mariachi band into a wedding reception & watched the bride & groom dance to the Mariachis. It brought tears to my eyes!

SUNDAY
12-30 8:30A   David said he rested fitfully & asked about another patient, Richard, that had coded. Richard was a bike accident (motor) victim & was "trying to die" according to the nurses.
The doctor came by & removed the collar. Davids pain is a seven in the abdomen. He is moderatly concerned & suggested a CT w/ Dye.
The leg swelling has reduced significantly & P was shown the injury. Wow! It is better than I anticipated. ~~More~~ He has a lot of skin and it looks good.
The 2 units of blood from last night gave him better

color.
His big complaint is the tube
& he tries to adjust it himself.
I asked if he wanted me to
read the paper & he suggested
the comics but they forgot them.
~~Wendy~~ is on duty again. She's
great.
I rubbed David's foot lightly & it
didn't bother him. I will continue
from time to time and remind him to
wiggle his toes.
Wendy adjusts the tube but
doesn't make progress. The night
nurse tried to get him off the
ventilator but he has medicine to
keep his blood pressure up & it
drops w/out the meds. He must
keep it up on his own to be
off. His alertness is not
helping so Wendy gives him some
morphine & cuts the BP meds in
half to see where we stand.

1100 A John arrives so I will
get a break Christi insists
on coming up even though
she sounds aweful.

David states that he "had a bath & it was wonderful." BP is holding...
I ask why the right foot is splinted. The nurse will check the chart, she thinks there is a fracture there as well.

1400 Sunday 12-30
David asked me (Christi) to call Malvern Center on Rte 29 to notify his group time at 6:30 AM of his condition (AA group)

I told David that we found the name of the paramedic Steve Rose, Jr from Station #1 Rescue 20 who took care of him. David will sign a card for him which we will deliver Monday 12/31 with one dozen steaks for the station #1. David was crying with joy.

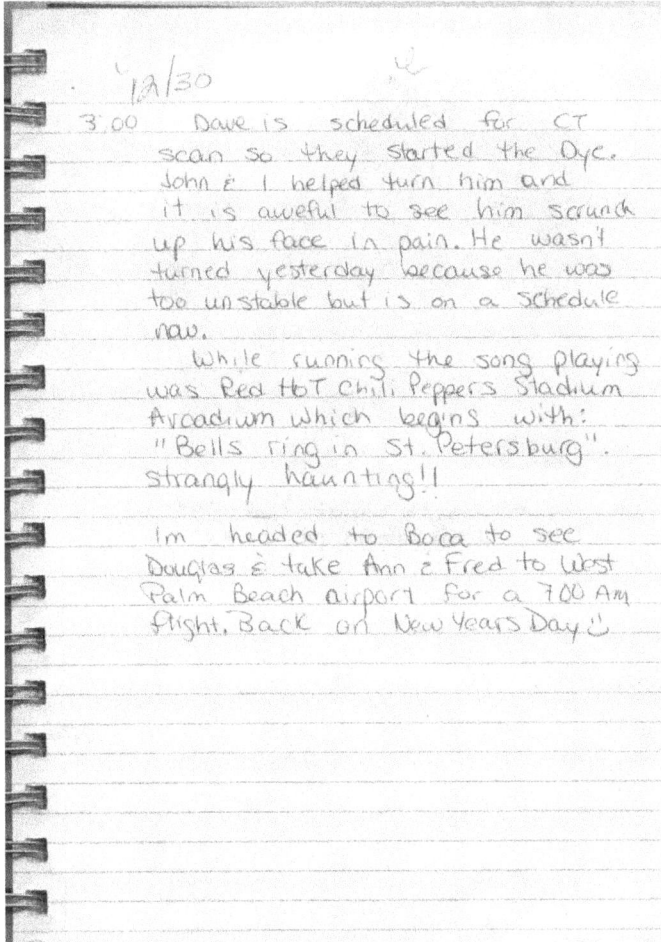

12/30

3:00 Dave is scheduled for CT scan so they started the Dye. John & I helped turn him and it is aweful to see him scrunch up his face in pain. He wasn't turned yesterday because he was too unstable but is on a schedule now.

While running the song playing was Red Hot Chili Peppers Stadium Arcadium which begins with: "Bells ring in St. Petersburg". Strangly haunting!!

I'm headed to Boca to see Douglas & take Ann & Fred to West Palm Beach airport for a 7:00 Am flight. Back on New Years Day ☺

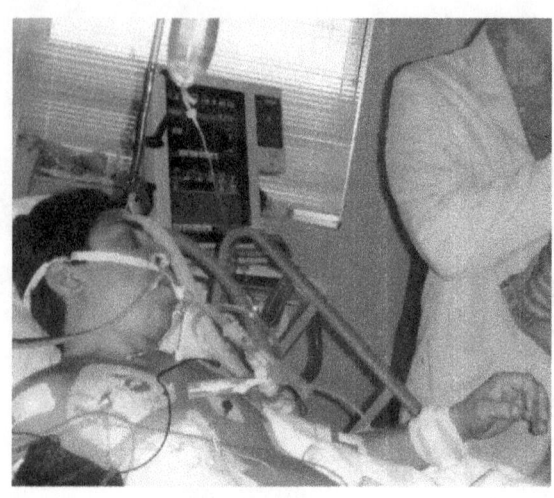

by Dr. Christine Gerbstadt
Taken 12/31/07

12/21/07

1145 HRS

72 hours sence the big nasty. David has shown incrediable strength and courage. This morning he asked me for paper and pen to draw with. Nurse Michel is taking care of him today.

Chrisie & Peter are on their way home from work, after stopping by the firehouse to give the people who saved David a coffe of steaks.

Sucsion - sucsion and more sucsion then morphine, then repeat. This is what Dave's life is all about right now. He's sleeping a lot today too.

12/31/07 and
midnight 01/01/2008
Peter + John Christi
brought in the New Year
with David, Now on NG
tube feedings (he passed
flatus) and Low grade
temperature. It looks like
a pneumonia is brewing

David had bad dreams all
throughout afternoon/
evening after getting
morphine. He is awake
now.

NEW YEARS DAY ☺ Tuesday
8:30 PM Visit:
Ugh! the drive is long but worth it and missing David for 2 nights was almost worth seeing the improvements. John has been too close to realize how far David has come. We arrived just in time for him to move his bowels into the bedpan. Wow, it was strenuous. Serious gas but his body will be running like a Porche soon. Temp is 101.4 I hope it comes down. David expressed that he wants to be an advocate for helmets & motivational speaker for mind healing. He says this experience has changed his life.
Peter & Sylvia were here waiting to see Dave when John & I arrived. They will pick up Marta at the airport & Sylvia leaves on Thurs. Lots of coming & going. John is tired & worried if he leaves he won't be able to come back and it could be months before he sees David.

I'm sure we will work something out.

Jan 2:
8:30 The nurses are busy in th ICU so I use the time to take care of business. Called dad with eye glass info. Called State Farm & started claim process - getting declaration page sent to attorney.

I called ICU at 4:30 AM & talked to Stacy. David was on bed pan every 1-2 hours.

9:30 AM - I finally get to see David! So many phone calls. I missed the rounds. Pulmonologist saw him & another Doctor said the splint would come off the right leg. Christi is concerned about fluid output of lungs. She is sick & working so she needs to rest & relax.

3:00 P. back to the hospital after a run & a bath & a jillion phone calls.

I will put their numbers in Davids new phone when we get it. John is stressed. I have a lot of compassion & concern for him. He is in that place of uncertainty & this is very confusing. I hope he can meditate & try to relax. Stress is dangerous & can wreck havoc on your body & brain!

Davids BP is lower than the AM 106/71 & HR is 91. He was higher earlier. His temp was down to 99.8° but feels a touch higher now.

I see from the machines that he is still at 40% O₂. Lung secretions are slowed down on the left side but the right side is still secreting. The nurses mark with a marker where the fluid is after their shift so I can check easily.

★

4:00 P. Respitory therapist suctions Dave he is on CPAP th until 7:00 PM & will be evaluated. Lungs are recorded as CLEAR yeah.

Dad calls and has new phone. glasses are 7-10 days out.

5:30 P. David is resting. He notions, I scratch. Shannon chastised me for coming in w/out calling.. but I did! Who? Chad!! ha ha bitch. I'm a rules' girl too & I'll win!!

headed out soon - back @ 8:30

1/2/08
9:00?
DAVES ASLEEP HE LOOKS LIKE HE'S DEEP
SLEEP. LAURA + I HAD DINNER AND
CAME TO BAYFRONT THIS EVENING.
I WAS NOT FEELING WELL THIS AFTERNOON,
SPENT MOST OF THE AFTERNOON IN BED,
WHILE LAURA VISITED

morphed up & out for the night. His
respirator is rated + back on Cpap
in AM
Right lung still secreting
Left lung no change for 12 hrs.
lung x-rays in AM.
Still no word on Right leg
possible fracture. Looks like soft
tissue to Dr. Laura
Night nurse is Stacey & was in
OR when admitted. She is
amazed at progress!!
  will call at 4 AM ☺
nighty night xxoo

1-3 Thurs
  8:30 AM
  The whole crew from when
  Dave was admitted is here.

They are AMAZED he's alive
& doing so well. It's plain to
see that this is what keeps
them going. Nurse Lynn is
great & the Respitory therapist
says if Dave stays rested &
calm w/ no problems they will
take out respirator. Wow so much
progress so quickly.
BP is 107/67
HR is 97
On Cpap w/ 40% O₂
left lung insignificant secretion
right lung about 50ml per 12hr shift
The nasty looking "food" is
disappearing.
- Today it was 34° !! Cold
There were "wind chill warnings"
which really made Jim chuckle.

3:00 - David is anxious and Lynn is
concerned. She brainstorms that
he is doing so well to reduce
his anxiety she wants to remove
the mask & switch to a cannula
David requests restraints, he is
having nightmares & worried
he'll injure himself. Lynn

explains there is nothing to damage. He expectorates fluid & suctions it out himself. She wants him to be self reliant so when he is stepped down he can do things himself. Lynn finds a fan to cool him off and gets busy cleaning & emptying. Gail stops by, she was the OR nurse when he arrived that I spoke to on the phone. She tells me she didn't think he'd make the night. She is so thrilled. She explains everything in detail. She sees the IVC filter drain and gets alarmed then explains to me how the Inferior vena cava filter prevents clots from going to his heart or head, ultimatly fatal. David is not on a blood thinner. Gail thought David would lose his leg minimally and is impressed by the vascularity & can't squeeze his warm toes enough. She lost her younger brother to cancer 2 yrs ago, age 49, & was so glad I made the trip.

    David complains about the BP cuff, it tightens

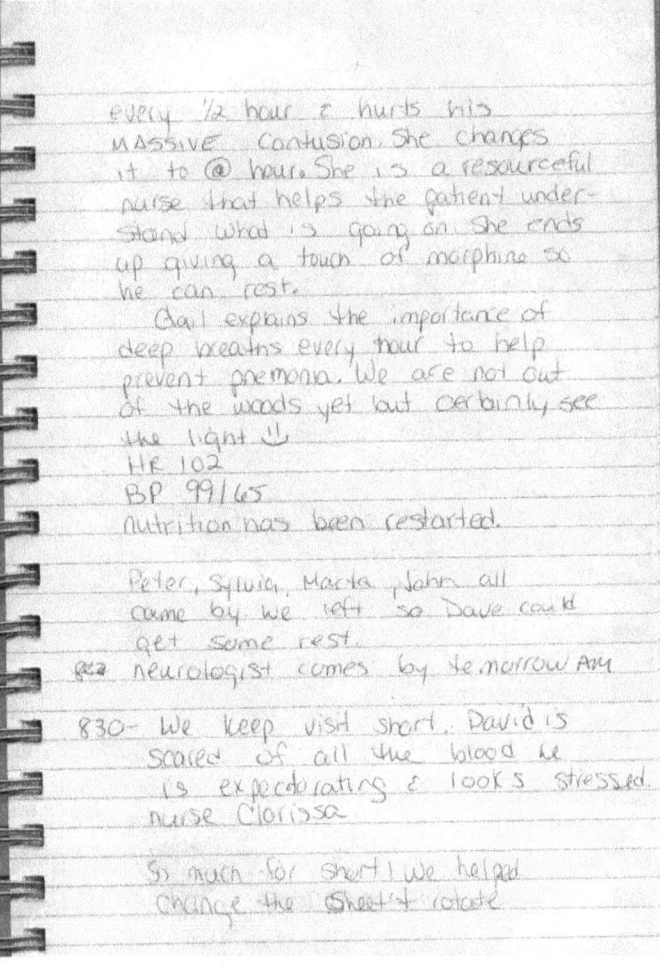

every ½ hour & hurts his MASSIVE contusion. She changes it to @ hour. She is a resourceful nurse that helps the patient understand what is going on. She ends up giving a touch of morphine so he can rest.

Gail explains the importance of deep breaths every hour to help prevent pnemonia. We are not out of the woods yet but certainly see the light ☺

HR 102
BP 99/65
nutrition has been restarted.

Peter, Sylvia, Marta, John all came by. We left so Dave could get some rest.
neurologist comes by tomorrow AM

830— We keep visit short. David is scared of all the blood he is expectorating & looks stressed. nurse Clorissa

So much for short! We helped change the sheet & rotate

David. He is still anxious. A little morphine helped us get the job done. O_2 saturation is about 98% until his anxiety or shallow breaths & coughs drop it to 90%. He can catch it up by breathing deeply. Chaplain Cyndi says a prayer.

FRIDAY JAN 4:
8:30A I woke up at 430 & called but no one answered so I figured they were too busy. Sleep was restless but worse for David, no doubt. He had bi-pap for a few hours overnight for a rest.
Nurse Carol has given David morphine & a laxative. He was given a respitory mask to help breath and removed it himself last night.
Things look good. BP 119/71
HR 101
O_2 100%
Vascular surgeon explains left foot drop could be result of sciatic injury

Peter already explained so I dont have a lot of questions. They will watch it but ultimately if the nerve has a lot of damage he could use a boot for dorsi-flexion.

The neurologist has not come by but they took more chest x-rays this AM. The "A" respitory therapist comes by. She is pleased with his strong cough & stronger voice. They all adore him!

10:22 - Tubes out. Carol gave little warning & a quick action, a pret

Saturday 1-5-08
John came by @ 9AM. Christi slept in + came later. David had a good night + looks like he rested. No BM for > 1 day but lots of gas.

We had lots of positive "ness" today:
① David's friend Mark from the Malvern Center sent his sister Tina in to visit. We found out she was Conestoga '74 (Anselmo)

Tina, David + Christi talked up Conestoga, siblings, reunions (making your own) and she left a care package with a card from the Malvern Center, lots of "Grapevine" issues and Pencils/felt tips + Pads of drawing paper. Oh, also M+M's.

David ate all of his breakfast + lunch (blended veggie soup, lowfat milk, 2 popsicles and juice + ice tea.)

David is taking Percocet for pain now + still has nightmares/flashbacks about the accident + other bizarre permeations of Reality. I asked Carol, RN if he could get a psych consult to help him deal with PTSD, depression and surviving a major trauma. David agreed it was like going through the stages of death + dying. Last night he was on the "Why me?" stage. He still struggles at times to stay with the here + now (especially when he closes his eyes.) So we've been watching cooking shows on TV to stimulate his appetite and keep him focused on the present.

John went to TPA to pick up Dad. Today is Douglas' Birthday 55. We can't wait to hear how his surprise party on the 65 foot motor yacht goes. I guess we will wait until tomorrow to not spoil the surprise.

David made his first (20) drawings last night to ease his mind after the Nerve conduction study by the neurologist. The report showed peroneal Nerve injury on the left, but it already appears to be repairing. The Neurologist started Neurontin for the shooting electric pains in his left leg.

DAVID'S JOURNAL

Note to reader: Journal entries have, for the most part, remained unedited to preserve my state of mind.

January 9, 2007   Day 12

The night was a mess. Sheets were everywhere. A chest tube and catheter were present along with some other stragglers. The nurse who attended me was spot on! I love a nurse that can just walk in a room, see a patient, and within 5 minutes have everything done and on to the next patient. Dan had been an army nurse and seen and done more than most nurses. He did his job with sharp and clean movements always smiling for he knew I would be transferred to general care floor and out of ICU. I kept saying, "Someone needs this bed more than I do!" "I can feed myself!" A huge step off the ventilator and feeding tube!

I knew it would still be a long time before I would be allowed to leave the hospital. Once out it would still take time to recuperate. I was one of the few that would leave this floor alive.

The orders came down. I would be leaving ICU. The chest tube was pulled out. Chest tubes are half inch in diameter and run one foot inside along your lung. Your told to breathe in and out three times, and in one fell swoop, the tubing is raised high above the doctor's head it feels similar to a huge bandage being yanked off at once.

The catheter was last. I griped the bed rails as I saw the nurse start to pull. With a continuous motion, the tubing all came out. Feeling like well tubing being pulled out your penis. Really not painful to be done. The nurse said, "Now you have to pee 300 ml in an hour. If you don't we have to put the catch back in." Coming out is easy. Going in well that is painful. I drank and drank. The nurse turned on a sink and let the water flow. "An old army nurse trick" he said. I peed the 300ml and then some.

Dinner came and I ate the wonders of hospital food. At about 9 pm I was transferred out of ICU!

I was transferred to another bed and wheeled up to the fifth floor. This floor was loud! Patients walked freely in the hall and in their rooms. Certainly no one was critical condition on this floor. My roommate had his back to me as I wheeled into the room. His neck was bandaged with a huge red spot of blood in the center. I would have his story repeated to me over and over. He was quite drunk.

My roommate had put his head through a glass window and nearly died. All night he kept asking for pain meds. I slept very little that night. I just thought, "Man you can walk and go to the toilet whenever you please!" I needed to call for a bed pan and be helped on. My roommate kept alcoholism very green for me. He was lucky to be alive, and too inebriated to know it.

January 10, 2007 Day 13

Several times I awoke through the course of the night due to my roommate's babbling and the general floor noise. I called this floor the cruise ship floor. The rooms were very small and tightly placed together. The patients all spoke loudly and it reminded me of a cruise ship. There was the patient across the hall with broken pelvis who I could hear quite clearly. Shouts for bed pans were common.

I was given a plastic tub filled with lukewarm water and various bottles filled with stuff to clean me and make me smell like a hospital. I asked for a mouth wash without alcohol and the nurse smiled and asked how much time I had. "Fourteen years." I replied. "Great!"

My roommate left at noon still a bit in the bag. Seems this was just another episode of his drinking.

My dad and my sister Laura came to visit, bringing me markers and pads.

Later the same day, another roommate came in. This time a car accident. He plugged in a video game system to the television. Another person was still in coma. One of the many I heard about in ICU.

My new roommate was quiet and considerate. No funny business was done during the night and I slept a couple hours. He went home after breakfast.

The afternoon was filled with the usual screaming, talking loudly, and occasional shouts for a bed pan or blanket. I drew and stared into space on the drugs that managed my pain.

While savoring my yummy dinner of some noodles with stuff mixed in, a nurse came in and said I would be getting a new roommate with a sitter. My first thought was would he be handcuffed to the bed too?

Turns out a 'sitter' is someone who watches to make sure patients that have high risk of getting out of bed and or ripping out their tubes don't! Sitters got paid to sit and watch patients. If they were caught sleeping, they would get in trouble.

This guy was a classic case of yet another drunk who found a way to land himself in hospital. Like all the rest of the drunks he was lucky to be alive. I called him Crushed Guy. All night he would wake up and try to rip out his tubes and get out of bed. "YOU DON'T UNDERSTAND I GOT TA' GO BACK TO WORK!" Man, the guy would sit up and try his hardest to get out of bed. I cringed at the thought of his situation. He kept it very green all night. He had three sitters through out the night. The last one told me about a family member who was in a car accident that passed four lanes of traffic and smashing into a building.

He told his brother everything happens for a reason. Now you are closer to god to show how loving and powerful he is! It was not his 'time' to die and he still had work to do. I told him about my accident. The man told me with pure love and kindness that I had special work to do and I must tell the story! You have a story to tell you must tell it.

In the very early hours of morning before breakfast a woman came to draw blood. For some reason I told her my story. She held my hand and said, "you have a story to tell you got ta' tell it." She repeated what she had said several times. I reassured her I would tell the story. She packed up her supplies and smiled at me as she left she said, ya' gots' a story ta' tell go an tells it.

January 11, 2007   Day 14

After breakfast the usual tub of lukewarm water came and the word that I would be being transferred to the 7th floor for rehab. I had been warned many times that the 7th floor was a tuff place. "Your gonna be in boot camp!" the nurses said. I thought it cannot surly be worse than what I have been through already bring it on!

Note: Here is first drawing I did. A self portrait drawn in pencil and colored pencil. At the top December 28, 2006 is the incorrect date. It should be December 28, 2007.

Saturday January 12, 2008

They wheeled me right up to my new room. My roommate an older guy who was in a car wreck that was not his fault. By far the best room mate during my stay.

Sunday January 13, 2008

Woke. Washed up. Before that used to be the most I did during the day. Now there is occupational therapy and physical therapy which means work. Just moving out of bed I am finding difficult. I came back from my workout and in my room was Laura's husband! Wow! He drove 4 hours just do bring a huge pile of mail to me. He even was fixing my lap top.

Monday January 14, 2008 Day 18

Had a BIG POOP last night! Slept excellent! Occupational therapy came in and helped me get dressed. Ate a big breakfast. The nurses down stairs were right it is boot camp for rehab. Will be here four weeks.

Tuesday January 15, 2008 Day 19

Not sure what to write this morning. Still dark outside. Just filled the bed side urinal with 400ML. Knocking off will write later... drugs taking hold. I may say it more than once I owe my life to station 1, the chopper pilot, doctors, nurses, the techs, everyone working here. Most of all I thank the gods, angels, and spirits for being closer to them.

Wednesday January 16, 2008 Day 20

7:45 am I have been trying to draw for an hour and find my self a few minutes later with pencil in hand. Drawing again and move pencil an inch or so and wake up a while later with pencil in hand still not any farther. Drugs are in full swing.
I wake up countless times to; pee, shift body, night mares, sweating drenching the sheets. I had blood pressure 98 over 40 scared the nurses. Two more nurses came in and took it again. Finally, it broke 110 and they left me sleep. Sometime later I felt my mom and missed her. Tears.

I know I have a story to tell. I feel such a dramatic story needs telling. By telling my experience, strength and hope I can perhaps help someone else heal, and know life goes on.

Today the nurse pulled out all the sutures and staples. Eight staples in stomach and 32 near groin on the scar I call the road map. I saved a staple and stuck it in my journal.

Friday January 18, 2008 Day 22

Woke up crying. Went back to sleep. Woke up crying. Back to sleep. Woke up. Dressed. Shaved. Breakfast.

To physical and occupational therapy I go.

Had 3 visitors today! First visitor today was the wife of a Colonel. She told me her husband was the Colonel was down the hall with a broken back and depressed. The Colonel heard about my story and wanted to talk to me. His wife came in as an introduction. I told her to try and stay in the moment. Take one day at a time. The colonel was transferred out the next day for sever depression. To think a guy who made the rank of Colonel wanted to see me for my courage and bravery! I never met him. We were all in the same boat as trauma victims.
The therapists said I was great for moral. Learning everyone by first name and cheering them on! I was the one that could not die. I had work to do and was going to do it!

The second visitor today was Tippy the dog. Tippy came in to my room and pressed his head against my bad leg and did not move. His heat drifted into me and made me feel good. I got to know Tippy over the next several weeks.

The last visitor of the day was Betty a pastor. She wheeled in my room with a joy-stick wheel chair and reached out her hand for me to hold. Tears came pouring out. She smiled. She would come every other week just to visit the patients and talk to us.

My gods give me what I need when I need it. Angels holding hands, smiles and love.

Saturday January 19, 2008   Day 22   (3 weeks + 1 day)

I slept good last night no pain. No bed sores. Today Christine my sister visits! Oh so happy! I woke up! I praise gods, spirits, and angels for giving me life. Ahhh! Passed out. Slept with pen in hand.

This morning we have nurse Salanra. Doctor on rounds. My vitals were checked. Then breakfast. Every morning it is the same way.

Amanda called me last night. We told her the whole story. She gasped a lot and just could not believe I was still alive. She especially wanted to know more about seeing the light. She said, "I LOVE YOU!"

I thought to my self... I loved her so long ago and never told her. I wanted to be with just her. I never told her how I felt. Somehow I knew it would never work out.

We are friends and she is one of my favorite living artists. She is happily married to Keith now. I am happy that she found Keith.

Now, far beyond the scars, staples, and metal rod it is the emotions I feel. I cry often when I tell the story. I feel safe in the hospital... On the outside not sure... I know I am not in the moment. Projecting the future is pointless.

Doctors, nurses, techs, call me a miracle. A miracle... Me? How am I to... How I am... Now is the time the tears come and words come that I can not say with out tears. "Am alive... I died." It all feels like a dream. All of this! But it is not. It is real. It's real alright. Fifteen to eighteen people on the rehab floor. There is one guy who was on a motorcycle at a stop sign. Someone ran the stop sign and ran into the motorcycle and kept going. Now, the motorcycle guy is missing some fingers and half his leg. He wore a helmet. He is a miracle as well.

I survived the accident now I have to survive the fact I survived. Today, I take each day as it comes to me. I cope with images and other triggers that release tears and horror that no one can expect to understand.

Sunday January 20, 2008 Day 23

Woke up. Dressed. Eat breakfast.

9:30 am Physical therapy for 1 hour. Back in my room by 11 am for a NAP. Then lunch. Then we moved to another room since our toilet was broken. It is funny because both of us in the room are on bed pans. So, we split and went to separate rooms. I liked Jim as a roommate. Quiet. Considerate, mellow.

I was moved to the motorcycle guy room. All the nurses told me he was a good guy to room with. The nurses had to get a big cart to move my stuff. "You got a lot of gifts and mail David!" She grumbled as she packed up my stuff. It bugged me she was so mad at me for causing extra work for her.

2:30 pm Occupational therapy. More jigsaw puzzles. I am able to do a 100 piece in about 20 minutes while standing. It helps with standing the puzzle distracts you and makes you stand longer. The puzzle also helps with fine motor skills, focusing, and problem solving. Then the therapists gave me a 1,000 piece puzzle to work on. Finished that in 2 days. Not bad for a trauma guy!

5:00 pm Dinner came I ended up leaving the chocolate cake and half the fresh apple. Calorie and protein in take is critical for healing. The body is burning off calories to heal and extra protein is needed for repairing damage to the body. Most times I get the yummy super dry fish or the special dried up beef.

6:30 pm I pooped! Oh boy that was a great poop on the toilet! Oh I am so happy I can get to the bathroom on my own and use the toilet! Seems all I do is eat, sleep, poop, and do therapy.

9:00 pm Usual meds come by via nurse. They seem to TRACK YOU DOWN! I have been in the laundry room washing my clothes all by my self. When the door opens and WHAM! There is a nurse with a cup of pills and a cup of water. How do they do it? I have searched my wheelchair for any devices and found none so far… I know they have a tracking device someplace… Maybe in my leg there are plenty of scars here. Hmm…
I joking tell the nurses this and they just smile and hand me the pills. I am on to them!

Off to bed about 9 pm cus well the drugs take effect somewhat.

11:10 pm Woke up crying from bad dream that is reoccurring. In the dream I am in an art class I have two pieces of art done and looking for the third one that is done. I can not find it! My sister Laura is trying to comfort me. I crumble one piece and crumble my self. It finally comes out that I say "I AM TERRIFIED TO FAIL!" I begin to cry.

I wake up crying. In the darkness I hear my roommate saying, "you will be alright."

Turns out he is on the phone and not aware of my crying. I make my dream out to be this. I do great art work I am afraid of being at CVS type job the rest of my life. As money is a symbol of being "successful artist" and it's not important. I am told Bob Dylan says, "you wake up do your day… what's money?"

Drugs are in me right now which, were prescribed by a doctor. I trust her. I only had one Percocet today for break through pain. Usually, I have four tablets. I do miss the other three inside. I want them. I am scared of returning to the outside world… Scared of people. How they will act towards each other, the world keeps on. In the hospital the focus is to save lives and get better.

I am scared of seeing my wound where the bones came out. Scared of steps and now often have reoccurring dreams of falling down steps. I wake from the dreams shaking and in terror!

Triggers of the accident lead to me crying. My emotions are fine-tuned to awareness of people and their roll or jobs they have. I am aware of my body more. I stopped biting my nails. Scared or overwhelmed is more like it. That so many people love me so much. Tons of cards, books, phone calls, and visitors from out of state.

My gods as I understand gods. I choose gods there are many gods, angels, and spirits. They love me! It was not my time. I have work to do! I ask the gods to guide me to do the next right thing.

Monday January 21, 2008 Day 24

Beyond Breakfast. Beyond teeth brushed. Beyond shaved face. I just want to find a place to be alone and have a good cry! I did not sleep well yet again so by 10:30 am I am nodding off.

When I woke up Elaine the Jamaican cleaning woman was cleaning my room. She looked up at me in bed. She came over to the foot of the bed. "You alright now dear?" she said. Staring back at her she knew. She just knew. I started crying and could not stop.

Elaine put down her mop smiled and said, "everything is going to be alright now." She started praying over me.

The tears and snot just gushed out of me!

Elaine continued to pray. Then recited psalms 100, 121, 91, 93. I continued to cry. She said to you have a bible? I could not answer her. She looked in my drawer and tray table and found nothing. I will be right back she said. Coming back in a few minutes with a bible in hand she gave it to me. I read the psalms she had spoken to me by heart.

She said, "god give you strength." And she hugged me and left.

I had gone to the edge and made it! This accident was a turning point in my art. George Braque had a head wound in world war I and left for dead. He took a while to paint again.

My work is not done yet! You have seen nothing yet!

Morphine trip:

I had plenty of hallucinations while on morphine. Here are just some of them.

All the concrete outside is replaced by rubber. Groups of us would be human balls. Bouncing down long steps laughing and having a blast! I was healed and running down with the rod in my leg in no pain! Bouncing off everything!

Tuesday January, 22 2008   Day 25

Had a good sleep. The routine would be: Sleep a couple hours. Wake up drink some juice. Sit up and wipe the sweat off all over especially my back with a towel. Lay the towel down over the soaked sheet and go back asleep for another couple hours. I would repeat this several times every night.

7 am: A tech came in and x-rayed my chest. So many full body x-rays I simply lost track of them.

Had breakfast in the day room. It is great to see more people eating together. We laugh, joke about the food and other stuff. Imagine stoke patients next to spinals laughing! We are all just happy to be alive! Each day we get to see progress of people oxygen tubes removed. Stoke patients heads are up and they are feeding them self. People going from blended food to solid food.

Back to room to brush teeth. Pooped the largest ever! It hurt. We take pain pills which stop us. Then we take iron pills that bind us up even more. We take more pills to make us go. The result is a small tree. Nurses ask us how many times we go each day. Yeah, I could go on and on about poop. It just feels so damn good when you can go! And then the ritual of washing hands after.

Off to PT and OT! Zooming down the hallway in my chair using the railings on the wall to increase speed and go easy on the arms. Warp speed! Nurses yell at me to slow down! I don't listen. The balloons add a nice flare tied to the back of my chair. Zooming past the room with nurses and doctors in a meeting. Later I find they all laughed seeing a guy zoom by the window and second later a bunch of balloons.

In PT I walk with the walker and do screeches. When I am done I can always spot my wheel chair. The one with the balloons.

Meet with the psychologist. Fearful of future. Need to write more. Need to draw more. Need to stay out of my head. Need to stay in the moment. Passing out... Sleep.

12:10 pm Pushed call button to see where my lunch is.

12:25 pm Nurse finally came. 35 minutes to eat lunch. Open faced roast beef sandwich. Tuff and dry would be to kind for this meal. Searching for an adjective none come to mind. Times up! Off to OT and PT.

PT: walking tired. In OT I played Wii a computer game with inner action remote control. I did bowling and got a 139. Then played baseball my third hit I wacked the ball to the warning track. I screamed I got a base hit!! Scaring everyone in the gym. I ran it out and got a triple. Played one inning and my arm got sore.

2:30 pm Therapy is over time to go back to room anyhow.

Called dad. And went to dinning room to write and draw. It's to dark in my room like a cave.

4:00 pm Back to room falling asleep.

5:00 pm Dinner.

6:00 pm Ice cream.

8:00 pm Drug time. Out cold. Wake up several times with shoulder pain. Move to loosen up.

January 23, 2008   Day 26

7:45 am All dressed. Slept well. Snored well. Pain in shoulder worse. Stretched and did some yoga to loosen up. Will stretch more today. In OT worked on puzzle. PT walked 200 feet with walker. Back in my room tons of mail and cards came.

Some thoughts for the day:

Tears cleanse the warriors wounds.

Why do husbands die before wife? Answer: They want to.

A violent event is like striking a bell it will go away.

Just do the work. Don't criticize just do the work.

Can not polish anything unless you have something to polish.

Steady patient persistent.

The art will come along.

Just pushing straight ahead and chance will take care of the rest.

You got life! - one of my favorites. A nurse said, no matter what happens remember you got life!

Spirit energy does not die it simply changes form.

Follow your bliss.

Let your self be slightly drawn by the strange pull of who you really love. It will not lead you astray.

Courage is doing what your afraid to do. Their can be no courage unless your scared.

6:00 pm: Called Jennifer talked about 10 minutes. Took me over a year to call her. Yes, I have liked her for a long time and never have I called her. Wanted to before trip to Florida. Wanted to while I was here. I got a tri-fold greeting card with many people signing it. She wrote we miss you. So I called her.

I put all my fear aside and dialed. Jennifer was happy to hear from me. Yes, I like her and I am ok if nothing becomes of it and she is a new friend. Right before she hung up she said, you know that drawing you gave me before you left. Yes, I said. Well I have it on my desk at work.

From now on I will not put things off!

I am scared of just going back to work at CVS. I don't want to return. I owe it to my self, my soul, to my gods, and angels to tell the story and share love and art to the world.

I CAN NOT DO THIS ALONE! I am worthy of being hired! Please I need help in finding my way to be a channel in being hired.

January 24, 2008 Day 27

Slept well. When I mean well with only a few times waking up from nightmares and sweats. Less is wonderful.

9:15 am First poop on my own with out help! BIGGEST POOP EVER!!! So much in fact it piled up way out of the water from the center of the bowl and went down the pipe. Over 2 inches in diameter. Painful. Two tone dark and light a kaki color. Phew!

9:30 am: Wheeled my self to OT using left hand and right leg. In OT they asked if I wanted to make my own breakfast. I said, "yes I want to make FRENCH TOAST!"

The quote of the day reads: If you can not be content with what you have then be thankful for what you have escaped.

The doctors, media, etc. call it PTSD post trauma stress disorder. I call it ugly and shit. Suddenly, out of no where at any time I begin to cry out loud.

Triggers and dreams can and does put me right back where to that moment where the tire rolled over my leg… I know I need to write this. To put me in society I don't know until I am there. Man first. Healing second. Art third. Must stay true to my craft, my gift, my love. Art = life + love + gift. I had to stay true if I did draw instead of holding the blood back I would never draw again.

Friday January 25, 2008 Day 28

My mind drifts as an artist: Thinking of painting walls of my house with rollers. Pure color- PINK!

Ate a light breakfast today. It is frustrating to see therapists working with patients sometimes. How they speak to them in a tone as if they are a child and they are not. I just ask if they treat them as people. I had to learn to just keep my mouth shut and let them do their job.

Today, we cook French toast for breakfast in occupational therapy! Yay! Ooo I love French toast. A nurse brought in a quart of fresh orange juice made from the oranges in her yard just for me.

In the kitchen in occupational therapy I was so happy sitting in my wheel chair making French toast. It looked so good! Wheeled back to the table spread jelly on the French toast. Oh it was great! I looked out the window to the rooftop of the building. I saw some machinery on the roof. Another bite of French toast.
Looking out I tried to figure out what I was looking out on the rooftop. It was the tail end of a helicopter. The blades began to move. Tears rolled down my face and I began to sob very hard. The helicopter was triggering sever trauma. I could not speak. My occupational therapist knew my story and soothed me she was wonderful. I was wheeled out of the kitchen. Just the sight of a helicopter… I gasped and felt the affects of post trauma take hold.

My therapist wheeled me up to a table that my roommate was sitting at. Still crying I slumped on the table numb. A game of trouble was put in front of us both. Before long we were both laughing and having some fun. The trauma had drifted from my mind.

After occupational therapy I met with my psychologist which eased my mind even farther. We talked about "feelings of process and triggers." I do not know what to feel. Feelings come and the scary part is I can not explain the feeling I am experiencing.

After I left the Psychologist we went to the day room where singing volunteers showed up and sang songs. I was the only one in the day room as they say a song called 'joy joy joy'. I got what I needed when I needed it.

I do not need to "make art" to have art heal me. Through my mind I can wander listening to art or see art to heal me.

I am really not hear… I am over the bay pass all the sailboats. I really am not here… I am someplace else.

12:30- Had lunch with Carleda, Jean, Pat, Elaine. Funny, and good to eat with people in community- Eat easier and faster. I'll trade you green beans for brownies.

1:00 pm- PT was to much wiped out after 45 minutes! Rested the last 15 minutes.

Saturday January 26, 2008   Day 29

Slept well. Only woke up once to dry off the sweat. Did wake up several times managed to go back to sleep. At 8 am I was still groggy. Strange to think that I slept well. At least I got a few hours.
I have been up most of the night watching the clock go around and around. Got up and had breakfast in the dining room. I force myself up and out of bed no matter how bad the night was. The thought of being in this dark and noisy room I call the 'bat cave'.

8:30 am – PT. Had a brake between every exercise. I sure needed a brake. The lack of sleep and quality of sleep is wearing me down. Not much chance to get a moment with out a nurse doing something to you.

9:30 am - In the dinning room writing. My second greatest escape besides the accident.

I listen to patients talking in great detail about collard greens. Since my stay here I have learned how to cook them. I tried eating them for dinner. I gagged from the salt level and the sheer mush. I could trade anything off someone's tray for a small dish of this foul smelling muck. Woman would gladly trade brownies for collard greens! I tried to explain where I am from they don't have collard greens on restaurant menus. They simply did not believe that they we not severed. "It's all how you prepare collard greens These here greens ain't toos bad now you hear. Mine are better," she went on. "These ain't bad."

I could tell you how many times someone would repeat the same exact sentence during a conversation. Just to humor myself I would say five and then would count to five as the person spoke. The funny thing was before long now I would starts talkin' like they be doin'. I actually started using ya'all. It just came out! Surely, I thought I gets my butt wooped but good ifs I talks likes dat north.

While drawing in the dining room, I called Ken to put me back out of collard green land.

Ken went on about 1981, living on 8th Ave. in New York, Aids, and feeling alone. I miss ken. I tried to picture him scared and alone wearing his usual baseball cap with his beautiful dogs. He makes me laugh with the stories he tells. His world he says is small. I identify with so much he tells me. Our long phone conversations are detailed and help a great deal by the end I forgot why I was so sad, lonely, or depressed. I have compassion for this man who pours out his heart to me trying to just live and be happy. I had to cut our conversation short due to the arrival of my lunch tray.

I find it interesting how I can start a whole table talking about just about anything. I listen as I ask one woman how she made her collard greens. Ah, honey I takes a big fryin' pan adds onions and shugar. I's cooks that down till all carmalized. Other woman would chime in sayin' hows' day start off... I puts in butter first. Another says, butter and salt. The conversation goes around the table back and forth. I dens adds da' greens. I love turnip greens says another woman. Love em! Beet greens still another woman. I smile and take notes. Listening to everyone go on and on about cooking and life thangs is so rich to me.

Chicken feet I love chicken feet says a woman. Chicken feet I's never had much of dem says someone next to her. They good fur suckin' says the first woman. A nurse dives right in and says 'I make my boyfriend Brunswick stew!' I makes it with chicken. What is Brunswick stew I ask. Oh my! It's chicken stew. I puts in left overs. Corn n' tamatoes. Later, I could not help but wonder what all goes in dis' here Brunswick stew. Turns out that the stew vary greatly but it is usually consists of a tomato based stew containing various types of lima beans or butter beans, corn, okra, and other vegetables, and one or more types of meat. To make authentic stew the recipe calls for squirrel or rabbit meat. You can substitute with chicken, pork, or beef. I think of the many squirrels living back at home in my yard. They have more fur on them than meat.

Pat, an older man who has retired from two jobs and been around the world many times over just starts talking about his dad going into the backyard and taking a chicken by it's neck and swinging it real hard in a tight circle. Pat says, "I remember that as a small boy… my dad would then hand me a dead chicken and tell me to pluck the feathers out.

I love meal time. We laugh. We feel each others pain. Cheer and encourage each other on. Admire and comment on the progress of each other. I will miss this when I am gone. The friends we all made during a brief moment when we really needed it. Yup ya' jist dost hears mush talkin' about fryin' greens or chicken feet at meal time backs home…

2:00 pm – Back in room. Mail came. A huge box with balloons and a teddy bear I named right away! Samuel the bear! Samuel is perfect. I love him so much! I tied him to my wheel chair with the balloons. I called my friend Gail for sending me Samuel to me.

10:57 pm – My head is clear. People ask me for the story. Sometime hard for people to take. A lot of people say they are thankful that I did not die. I lived. Escaped death so many times in less than nine hours. The trauma that is stored in my head is nothing anyone can understand… except for someone who has had extreme trauma. I must be with these types of people like my friend Robert Ely he is one of my saving persons in my life.

> "A pessimist sees the difficulty in every opportunity; an optimist sees the opportunity in every difficultly."
> Winston Churchill

Note: Landscape pencil drawing looking out the day room.

Sunday, January 20, 2008   Day 30

Breakfast. I am fighting today deep hard post trauma stress at the moment. George Braque was shot in the head during World War I and found just in time to be saved. He took a long time to make art again. Fellow painters and critics did not think much of Picasso. They did regard Braque as a wonderful painter much better than Picasso. I want love of a good artist.

I am scared of leaving the hospital. Comfort zone.
I am scared of failing at a new job.
I am scared of trying a new job that I would love.
I am scared of asking women out who I like. Not scared of rejection scared of talking to her face to face.

I used to be more out spoken.

I have lost some things…
I have gained some things…

What they are… more than physical that doctors or money can not help with.

Phew. I say that a lot when I am alone. I escaped death. Only to be thrown back to society which I never felt as I belonged. The last part of 'out of Africa' comes to mind yet again.

Monday January 28, 2008   Day 31

I write this morning, "Just scribble if you think you can not draw."

Panic swept over me. The worst panic in a while. I lost my journal. I searched everywhere… in the gym, my room several times… everywhere. I became depressed… very depressed. Several nurses came into my room and asked if I was ok. I told them I lost the journal and they put that I lost my journal in my chart. My doctor came concerned and told the staff to keep an eye out.

I gave in. The journal is lost. I had to accept this and turn it over. Tossed and turned in bed...

Tuesday January 29, 2008   Day 32

Breakfast. Depressed. Journal gone. I looked in the FedEx box stuffed some mail that could not fit on the walls... There jammed in the box was my journal!

Holly smokes! This book is my pour out. I don't use this writing in my blog. Post trauma kicks my head! It is feelings I never had experienced before not able to put it to words. This is common with others I have read about with ptsd.

A friend of mine emailed me today, he said he chaired a meeting and used some of my emails as material. Someone shot up a hand and asked if they had gotten permission from me. I understand if my story was too much for people to handle.

I told my friend when I get back and tell my story it may very well gross some people out big time. So many topics; story full of blood, shit, white light, blood transfusions, tubes, nearly losing my leg, and emotions will spill out all over the place if it is told.

Now, my roommate and girlfriend are all mushy. He asked her dad for permission to marry his daughter. Yes, it seems I am gossiping here a bit... I am jealous a little. He is 31 with 2 kids from another marriage. Marring her cus' this accident changed "everything". She has been talking all night as though she is 5 years old.

I am 39 with out anyone – Yes, I feel lonely. Feeling sorry for my self? No, way. I did not get this far to feel sorry. Blessed is the word to be among the gods. Humble and be patient she is out there waiting.

I can paint for a life time be among hundreds of paintings, drawings, have plenty of comments. Love I can not create. I have to wait for love.

Good day no matter what happens…

Today we had OT at 9 am PT at 10 am Shrink at 11:30 am. Sisters came at about noon for a little while and then left. Then to PT walked 2 times. 1 short 1 long walk about 400 feet total. Wiped me out! Back to bed. Sisters came back at 4 pm. They woke me up and took me outside we sat in the sun and followed it as it moved….

To be with both sisters in the sun was a blessing. Back inside dinner. Meat balls and bow ties. BLAH! Shovel it down! Keep shoveling! Samuel my bear is my wing man! He is there while I eat, sleep, ride in my wheel chair… he is dare fur me! I love him!

This was a good day! No, matter what happens… "it's a good day!"

Got on the phone from 5 pm straight till 10 pm – 7 phone messages and while returning calls 2-3 different people call in for each returned call.

One of the calls sticks with me. I had called a friend Tony every day leaving voice messages with out him calling back… Tony had gone out hard on a binge spree I did not know about. On the third message I left with Tony he got… Just a 'hey man how you doin' give me a call back ok later.' Turns out he picked up this message got a moment of clarity and called someone to take him to a rehab. The next day I got a few calls saying it was my call that brought him back. I just was in my hospital bed I didn't know and learned a simple gesture can save a persons life. It was done for me with the paramedics and I was deeply honored I could return the blessing for Tony. Got me to be right sized. Even though both my feet are extremely swollen. The swelling and numbness in my leg will probably be there for 1 year. Oh, well I feel good.

Wednesday January 30, 2008   Day 33

To be in my hospital room is as though your on a bench for the New York City subway station. Yes, it's that noisy when the tube transport system is used day and night. Between that and sweating out my sheets several times a night. Up today at 5:50 am at   6 am a nurse comes in and gives me my pills. Breakfast is not till 8 am 2 bowls of oatmeal, an apple, 2 cranberry juices, and a coffee cake.

Today, I won't quit! Toughness comes in all sizes.

Laura and Christine came to day for family training. They learned how to transport me from wheel chair to a car.

I did go to an A.A meeting last night. The only people there was I, the woman who wheeled me there, and the guy who chaired. Such a big hospital and only 3 people. Half of the time was the chair talking about him when he was young. He was riding his 10 speed bike in St. Petersburg in a bad spot of town on his way to see a girl. He was jumped by a bunch of guys with base ball bats. They left him in the street with the bike on top of him. He was in coma for 10 days. All his left ribs were broken... and left for dead not even robed. He lived. Almost drank over all this. He stayed sober!!! He chairs this meeting here most times no one shows. The most I saw was 6 people. The guy just is there case anyone needs a meeting. He meets with a brain injury group. I learned that no matter what happens... I can not drink or use. At 14 years this trauma injury is the hardest thing... harder than stopping drinking and staying sober. I must return to my home group... I need them and they need me. My recovery will be easier.

Thursday January 31, 2008   Day 34

Slept uneasy the tube system kept me up. Rattles the walls and ceiling all night.

8:00 am – Breakfast. I am realizing that I space out and sleep. Or should I say pass out right in the middle of writing, drawing, etc. I want to see if I sleep better at Christine's house.

My roommate I feel is depressed. He stays in bed with the television on asleep or not. Stays in bed most of the time. I can not be around depressed people it makes me even more depressed than I am now.

I should be happy? Smile! I am not. People tell me to smile. When you have sever trauma in side your head with side effects of ptsd depression takes hold of you. Right now I have acute ptsd if it lasts more than 6 months then it turns into ptsd. I do what I need to do to fight it. Crying out of the blue for no reason, depression, extreme frustration, being hard on my self, night mares, night sweats, triggers; like helicopters, bicycles, reading and seeing trauma cases, and the worst part feelings I can not describe. For me ptsd sucks! I cover and stuff the crying usually in front of my family to protect them from crying as well. It seems to eat me up at times. Since I saw the accident it makes it harder… like my friend who was a sniper in the military he was "there" killing people and watching guys die in his arms… You can not know unless you have experienced something like this.

Visual and sound triggers of choppers flying by my room window all day and night… Right now I need to call someone!

Talked to my friend Robert. He helped clear my mind. Crying and coming off the edge.

PT and OT went well today. Also, talked to shrink about leaving for a short visit outside. I was scared I might cry in public. She said, "if you cry then you cry just let your self go through the feeling and know it's ok to cry!"

She is right it's better to get it out then have it inside… As the nurses say, "better out than in". Talked more about my roommate. He is depressing sleeping in and staying in bed all day watching television. I tell her I can not be around depressing people. My roommate back home… I go on and tell my shrink that I feel I can not heal and get better if he is there. I want my home for me. She agreed it would be best to have my home to my self. I leave the shrinks office releaved and stronger knowing I can cry and it's ok!

My sisters meet me and we leave he hospital for lunch. I am excited and scared.

The lunch went well. Great food at Friscos in St. Petersburg right next to vioto hotel. Had a fantastic piece of fresh seared tuna on top of azto with grilled veggies.

I had to go use the toilet after lunch. The waiter and staff led me to the restroom. They opened the door and helped me in. I got on the low toilet ok. The leg started to hurt pinched nerves. The staff banged on the door several times to see if I was ok… They were told the story and were concerned about me. I yelled back, "I am ok!" I thought what was bad was this extremely painful bowel movement! When done though boy oh boy! What a great bowel movement! My it was a revolution! Got a second wind! Ripped and ready to go! I wheeled out of there smiling and yelling let's go!

Friday February 1, 2008   Day 35

Today my roommate leaves. He has been here 14 weeks. Yeah, that is a long time. I hope it works out for him I wish him well… I mean it. He has been through enough.

Laura came for a visit at about 2 pm during PT. It is always good to see someone from the outside. After PT she and I go outside for some air! Oh I just love leaving the door and feeling the air on my face. Feels so good.

Back inside, I take a nap and woke up crying. Big water works.... Called several people. Got a hold of Ruth and talked for 1 hour during the call I continued to cry! It finally stopped and then I began to laugh! So, wonderful I have Ruth in my life.

I think of other patients who do not have support systems. I got to take care of me! David! I look at the cards covering the walls and smile a little knowing I am loved.

I said, out loud "Ruth done help me... oh my I did say done help! Get me out of the SOUTH!"

Saturday February 2, 2008   Day 36

"Sock it to me cake"

Just because you are a Christian does not make you a good person. Someone told me this in the dining hall and it fits perfect for any religion.

Finished a 1,000 piece jig saw puzzle by 1pm today. I find that puzzles are a good way to clear the mind and eliminate the element.

What is it with people in the south? They say "good" in stead of well. It used to "bug" me then it became comical just knowing when the person would say well amused me. Also the line I heard during dinner one night. A woman saw something on the dining room television. It was a cooking show... A woman eating next to me said, they are not tellin' me notin' I coulds use... They not making collard greens or frying something." Then she said something I nearly choked with laughter... The woman said, "you would eat a worm if I gave it a French name". Oh boy! This is coming from someone who puts mayonnaise in her grits along with butter. Oh yum! And you wonder why her knees are being replaced.

The rest of the day consisted of eating the standard meals, watching bad television, drawing a little, and writing. I am content on just doing this. Writing is becoming something that must be done.

Honesty, I am glad my mom is dead. I would have hated to see her suffer. I did see her several times in ICU while on morphine. She was standing there dressed in a beautiful outfit sharp as ever. Smiling at me. I got the sense that she said, it will be ok. I love you David. 'I love you mom!'

Sunday February 3, 2008   Day 37

"We have bananas today!"

Called Jennifer today. She seems very excited when I call and Robert tells me she is extra excited to know if she got any drawings from me. I believe she likes me… That is good cus' eyes' likes her. (ok david you gots' ta' get your butt outs from dis here south befur it's to late!)

At this moment my mind is clear at 37 days. There are things I have seen and felt that have changed from the moment the artery was cut and blood flowed onto the pavement… I fought for my life… My friend who was in a war and saw plenty of guys die in his arms with the same wound as I had. Of all the guys he saw no one survive.

I can tell you 37 days in… yes I escaped death and was kissed by many gods. That day Steven gave me CPR in route to hospital. My heart stopped 2 more times in the hospital… 3 codes and a held artery.

So, now I lie here with thought of never procrastinate or put "things". I put off calling Jennifer for 1 ½ years until I just did it. Don't hesitate. Do it. I am not the same person as before December 28. I want to be happy. For me ptsd smacks back and takes happy away.

I am going to make Jennifer a valentine. Going to fight and get better! I must not give in and roll over in bed… I know that spiral of depression and I choose not to go there. Must maintain as an artist. Must maintain as a man. Must just be patient and kind to my self. Healing takes time.

Tonight Tom's mom called me on my room phone. I was in my wheel chair half way to the toilet. I told her to call me back. She did. She talked a bit. She said, "you can come to me for therapy sessions when you get home I take insurance".
I thought no way I am being solicited by her. Then said, Tom is here with me he wants to talk to you. He gets on the phone, "hey man guess you don't want to talk about the accident?" I tell him, "I prefer if we didn't" (duh!) He went on about the usual stuff I know what he does… I want to send you something in the mail. Ok I said here is the address. OH no that is ok I can look it up. I can give you…. He cuts me off no it's ok I will look it up don't trouble yourself. I tell him he won't be able to find the address and he does not know my room number. You can't just put the hospital name and my name. He gave in and took the address. (I did not expect anything and still have not gotten anything from him) Thanks for calling, I hung up the phone.

I lay there in bed getting mad! Got out of bed and paced the room in my wheel chair. Why was I pacing?! Anger kicked in. 5 weeks and 2 days go by and Tom's mom calls me and says Tom is here… What a useless person! As useful as a wet fart! I have lived with this guy for 3 years now and no call or email to see how I am doing. Just would like some compassion. Oh we IM'ed only because I happen to be online at the same time. Thoughtless, can not rely on him. I was HOT!! I called a few people I can't stay mad it's not good. No one answered the phone. I called my brother and spoke to him for 1 hour. Great conversation! Brother said, "you know David he has no idea how bad it is… and just doesn't have the skills to be compassionate". He helped defuse my anger and I felt great!

Monday February 4 2008 Day 38

7:15 am – Woke up. Still have a little anger. Told my doctor about it. I can't trust my roommate to do anything. I must kick him out of my head! To hell with him.

Anger I learned is part of ptsd. I recognized it and took care of it. My brother was a huge help. I just had to reach out and talk about my anger. Tom can not stay inside my head so I kick him out. He does not even have a clue I am angry with him. Nor does he have a clue about a lot of things. I found out who my friends are. As for his mom nice she is I just don't want to deal with people if I don't have to. Rather not write or think about those two anymore.

Breakfast = yogurt. Eggs, banana, and milk.

I want to call Jennifer today. I think of her a lot. Walking into the room and seeing her smile makes my whole day. Makes me feel as though everything will be all right. She has told me she cries a lot. I told her I do to. I could sense a sigh of relief over the phone. I called her Sunday she said she was just about to call me. I admit I like her. If she has no interest that is o.k. with me.

Spoke to Christine about Tom. Seems a good step would have him leave the house.

I CRY. I DON'T KNOW WHY I CRY I JUST CRY.

What it's like for me at the moment: braces on legs, stat checks every 4 hours, pills, peeing into a plastic urinal cus' I can't just stand up and walk the 15 feet to the toilet.

Crying. More crying. Anger. Frustration. WHAT THE FUCK IS GOING ON IN MY HEAD!

THIS ALL SEEMS SO SURREAL!!!

What do I do? Oh fuck the statement: "do the next right thing!" Christine is going through tuff stuff crying. We both are stressing – badly! So much on our shoulders.

Tuesday February 5, 2008   Day 39

TEARS. I feel I can't go on… I don't want to die. It all seems a struggle – Today is a day I was starting to cry and the nurse comes in to say it's time for breakfast. You want to eat in bed or in the dining room. I said, in the dining room! Really, I just wanted to be left in bed and have a good cry! Off to breakfast I go with swollen eyes. Doesn't matter everyone is so much in pain or got something on their minds they never even notice such things… Plus, they do it too.

Laura showed up a little before noon as I woke from a nap. OH I WAS SO HAPPY TO SEE MY SISTER! I HUGGED HER TWICE AND NEARLY CRIED HOLDING ON TO HER. She brought lunch and we ate outside. Oh a huge roast beef sandwich from a great deli nearby. Oh I needed the protein for healing and it tasted wonderful. MMM.

1:00 pm PT and OT. Had dinner inside. Laura stayed for dinner leaving shortly afterwards. I like having visitors I just don't like them leaving.

A nurse gave me a shower tonight! First shower in 1 full week. Normally, a nurses showers me every other day. I just kept being passed up for some reason. It took me some time to get used to a nurse washing me. May sound GREAT! Take in account the scars, trauma, and sad that I am not able to wash my self. The process takes some time: I wrap a towel around me and sit in my wheel chair wearing a robo boot on my right leg so I can stand on that leg.

Then I get wheeled into the bathroom. Inside, I hug the nurse and she picks me up out of the chair and pivot on the robo boot leg. The other leg I can not put any weight on. I am placed onto a plastic shower chair with hole in the seat.

The robo boot comes off. The nurse then sets the water. I can only take it very hot. Sprayed down. A wash cloth is laid on my right thigh and some green soap is squirted on the wash cloth. I take the cloth and wash my legs as far down as I can go, my chest and arms. This is an improvement though. She used to wash me all over from head to toe. Now, she scrubs the rest of my legs, back and head. She then stands back and sprays me down... Humbling experience for me. You think I would get some pleasure out of it. Instead, I feel very helpless and vulnerable. Seeing my leg scar where the bones came out took many weeks before I could look at it with out cringing and getting depressed.
The nurse then dries me off and we replace the robo boot and get wheeled out to fresh clean sheets. At least I will be clean and dry for a little while before I sweat out the sheets again.

Today, I finished the 550 piece jig saw puzzle I started a day or so before. So, what started out as a crappy day ended GREAT!

Tomorrow Laura comes early and we will go out for lunch for MEXICAN FOOD! Oh boy I can not wait!

Wednesday February 6, 2008

I feel scared to leave the hospital! Laura pushed me to the first street corner and I cringed, became nervous, and started flashing back to the accident. I sucked it in and fought back the tears. I did not want Laura to get up set.

Tonight would be tons of choppers going past my room and landing on the roof of the hospital. I am so thankful I can write this – with out brain damage – no spinal injury – no face scars – I got all my fingers and toes. I am ready to know why I was saved to live on! I want to know answers. I love myself... I have a crush on Jennifer. Have now for one and half years now. She told me on the phone that it stinks that it took an accident for us to start talking. She is shy. I am shy around her. She is thoughtful and kind.

She said, "when you get home we have to hang out together." After she said that she said, oh I got to go bye. It made me happy to know I would have a new friend when I got home. I figure it must have taken a lot for her to say that.

Even if she is not interested in me… the fact is I called her with a head full of trauma and talking to her makes me happy.

Thursday February 7, 2008 Day 41

Cordia, Gladys my good eating buddies are going home today! I started to cry… I told Gladys that I'd miss her she said, "she was not leaving me in spirit."

Sad I am sometimes when patients strike a cord with me and they leave. Gladys was one of the shining gems. She made me laugh at every meal. Such sharp quick comeback lines and quick jokes.

Laura and I went to Red Masa restaurant which was o.k. nothing great.

Called Jennifer she loves Mexican Food and is learning to cook. Rock! I came back to my hospital room to a box 3 foot square with 12 balloons. Plus, a card from Jennifer. I just started reading… and broke down crying! Wheeled into the hallway crying. Nurses came running up to me. What's wrong David! I hand the card and several nurses hug me. I just was so over whelmed by the generosity of people.

I miss my friends who sent me the box.

I miss Jennifer. She I beautiful. Her smile makes me smile and be happy.

Friday February 8, 2008   Day 42

Woke a bit before 8 am (today is 6 weeks)

Washed face. Felt great. Thought of Jennifer. Happy Day! Good PT getting easier. I want to do a series of paintings for the floor. 1- never give up. 2 – you can do it. 3 – Try.

My lawyer came today. Best to have a good one. He is wonderful. Just figure on details no problem.

Gladys left Thursday sad my buddy is gone. She had a hip replaced. We laughed and joked. She was in her 80's had great 1 liners to crack people up and smile… We shook hands. I said goodbye… she said, she was going and leave a little of her sole. I miss her… 4 more left today. The people just slip away and never heard of. Quiet… New people come… I remain. I have gone through 5 roommates already.

Friday nights I speak to my dear friend Ruth. Wonderful to have her in my life again. I am so happy and going to run with it. I know it won't last… Jennifer brought joy and happiness when I needed it. I have enjoyed her smile.

Everything will be o.k.! The truck did not stop me it just slowed me down.

I wanted to go down to ICU… and see my old room. Leslie my PT took me down. Ken was down there… The nurse that had me the last shift. He was an army nurse and had seen more than I care to mention. We shook hands and told me to walk around… It all was unbelievable to be on the other side of the bed. We went past every patient and went back upstairs.

Saturday February 8 2008   Day 43

NUMBER 43 – Life, universe, and everything.

7:15 am woke up. 7:30 am out of bed! Feel refreshed from speaking to Ruth. I escaped what we call tragedy and died an it was powerful. After that I came back. My life is a miracle.

My cell phone I lost it! I start looking for it… I tell the person I am speaking to on my cell phone I am looking for my cell phone… oh I just found it… in my hand. Then I thought I lost the pen cap to a good pen. The pen I found in my hand with the top on the end… When you go looking for a pen check your hand and the end for the top.

It is hard… I am learning to shut up and not stick in my body to "help" when help is there as a professional… I only get in the way.

I am HAPPY! Why? What is the formula?

I slept ok. Woke up 1 time for sweat drying with bath towel. Wiped my back and bottom soaked and sheets. Put a towel down so I could sleep on something dry.

Spoke to a few good friends about life and falling in love. I prayed lying in bed. Thank you prayer - thank you paramedics, helicopter pilot, doctors, nurses, techs, brother, sisters, dad, cleaning woman, therapists, friends by name… and I continue naming all those I can think of. Got out of bed with a good clear head and wheeled to the laundry room for clean clothes.

Simple tasks I can do on my own: washing clothes, using a flush toilet, shaving, cleaning self, etc. are tasks that may be hard if one can not do certain tasks. I don't have to call a nurse for a bed pan and slide it under me. Better yet I don't mess my bed anymore. Which is really no big deal. A nurse can clean a soiled bed in a few minutes. Rolling the patient to one side wiping up the mess off the patient. Sheets are gathered up and new sheets are slid in. Patient is rolled to other side soiled sheets are out and clean is rolled back. Done!

In ICU with unconscious people on ventilator like I was… Soiled sheets rates as a low priority. Lower than say a ringer going off if a patient has a low pulse rate or blood pressure or a stopped heart.

My alarm went off for low blood pressure. Another time for low oxygen not long after I was taken off the vent. The nurse put a mask on me. When I breathed in it would push air in me – it had to be adjusted I could not handle it. I had to relax and really focus on breathing and get used to the mask. For 1 hour I was given this… Yes, tubes came out… IU was removed, then off oxygen. Yes, bones mend. Yes, my mind remembers a lot. I must take care of my mind as well.

I am considering writing a book… Titles come to mind: 1 breath at a time… The book would have drawings, letters from friends, etc. I don't want to profit from this accident with a book – need to really focus on purpose "why doing" – "motive" – should I write this? I asked my lawyer, he said he does not attract attention with his cases. He told me I had the right to write a book… Best he said, to do it for "me" and journal. Which I have been doing.

Perhaps I am looking for "permission" for me to do this book. I woke with the idea. To just write. What style? Form? I just got to write and not worry of style or form. Perhaps I made my discussion… If it helps me good. If this book helps just 1 person then it was all worth it.

The 7th floor dining room looks over the bay at St. Petersburg. Straight ahead a small airport where dozens of small planes land and take off. It's a busy place. Next, to that is a small harbor with sail and power boats even a coast guard cutter. The sun rises above it all and brings warmth and light for all living and dying things.

Then a staff member closes the blinds and blocks off the sun. The sun is in the patients eyes. We can not look out now. Powerless. This guy has been working here 19 years… 19 years… I should write the book! Who cares if it takes 1 year or more…

Life changing for ever! Died. Brought back. I want to thank Steven and the paramedics for getting their hands bloody and saving my life. For that no words can be written.
Slept from 1pm to 3pm.

Dinner at 5pm. Called Jennifer. Miss her smile. She called me. O.k. I do believe she cares about me. My life will never be the same…

I do not want to work at CVS any more. I want to work with kids, art, and be paid. I have had so much time and have done nothing but dream about it. I need to do action! Now is the time to do it. Do I really need Trudy that art agent to rep me? No way!

If I return to CVS… I feel I failed… I can not let that happen! Art I do makes so many happy… I am worthy of being hired. One agent's rejection is not going to stop me!   Never give up! Keep going! I look at the hundreds of cards and letters on the wall and piling up! I will use what I got and build on that! I am not a failure! Just because I am not famous – I am not a failure because I am not rich – I am not a failure because I say so!

I was told it would be impossible! I did it my way! I stayed true to self and people love me. People love my art. Writing and finishing a book and speaking to the public… Yes! Become a motivational speaker! Never give up! Never give up! Walt Disney went to 300 plus banks for a loan for Disney land… before he got the loan. I won't give up!

Sunday February 9, 2008 Day 44

I woke. Still waking up! I ate. Rehab. Lunch. Dad visit. Rest. Rest. Rest. Toilet. Dinner. T.V. Draw. Write. Think. Draw. Movie. Dad Left at 7:55pm. Hug. Tears. "NO WEEPY STUFF!" dad says… He did not want to cry in front of me or on his 1 hour drive to my sisters place. Tears cleanse the warriors wounds.
I must tell my story.
I must not lie.
I got life.
Sleep.

Monday February 10 2008   Day 45   (1 ½ months)

I asked what people put on their grits:

Butter, mayonnaise, sugar, salt, milk.

I watch and listen to what people say at meal time:

Someone puts corn chips on a ham sandwich.
Someone puts jelly on eggs.

Then the conversation at lunch turned to: Being in a turkey prison, Nassau prison.

Someone else said today: That they moved half way around the world to live in Florida. When I asked them where they used to live. The person said they lived in Pennsylvania.

Then I was wheeled down to x-ray after lunch.

1:50 PM 0T- The orthopedic surgeon who put rod in my leg came by and said, "you should be dead". He then took off my braces and started stretching my leg out. He then said, all braces to be kept off and weight baring as tolerated on left leg.

2:00 PM PT - Leslie put me on the parallel bars and had me walk up and back twice. Then she put me on the stationary bike and I rode with out resistance for 11 minutes. Then she had me walk about 50 feet with the walker. Left ankle is extremely weak and I am afraid to put weight on the foot. By the end my feet are sore, stiff left leg and knee. I called Christine and she was so excited she went out and bought me sneakers!

3 pm to 5 pm – Nap. Christine and dad came and brought the shoes! I called more people to let them know I started walking with both legs.

We ate dinner in the dining room and watched bad television. I called more people.
Back in room my roommate was yelling at his girlfriend who was bathing him in bed. Anger. Fear. I must stay humble.

Tuesday February 12, 2008 Day 46

8:00 am – Woke up. Today, left leg is stiff. Stiff knee. Weak ankles. Life here in hospital is on going. The stats say that the Emergency Room handle 4,000 patients per month. I was just 1 of 4,000 in December.

Doctors and nurses keep telling me I should be dead. I have a second perhaps – more look on life. Few have been where I have been and are now. With only a few people I know. We help each other through.

I hide my crying from family so they do not suffer. In telling someone I know who has pstd this. They tell me that they do the same thing.

I asked my dad repeated if he was o.k. he would say, "I AM
FINE! I AM FINE!" I knew he was not "fine". A couple
weeks later I asked him and he said that he was scared the whole
time. My sisters and brother were torn up.

Time takes time...

The answers will come in writing and making art.

Wednesday February 13, 2008 Day 47

Doctor Williams tells me I may go home Saturday. Still painful
when I walk. Today in PT we tried going up and down stairs. I
have had nightmares about stairs and falling down them waking
up shaken and sweating.

Leslie helped me with the stairs and I did o.k.

So many thoughts of leaving the hospital. Bay Front Hospital
has been my home for almost 2 months. I cried, begged for pain
to go, counted the hours till daylight for countless nights...
Complained about the food.

Now, with possible release does not seem real... as my dad
turned and left...I wheeled my chair to my room door... He did
not get more than a few feet away... He can go. I stay. I nearly
cried... cried for not being able to show anyone what I
experienced...

I try to sleep. Sleep is hard for me... Scared for nightmares.
Then I wake up in the same hospital bed. More pills.

My roommate is getting to me. Must I write about him so
badly? His girlfriend is calling him on his shit. He is just full of
anger. Cursing out his girlfriend with a new baby. The yelling
got louder and heavy so I left the room. At 8 pm she stormed
passed the dining room where I was watching television carrying
her 2 month old baby.

She keeps coming here to hear her boy friend put treats and demands on her. "You be here at 4 pm!" When she calls and says she can't make it. He flips out with cursing and shouting. I can't stand it and leave the room. After his girlfriend comes and goes... His wife shows up with 3 kids.

This place is like a daytime television show.

Here is what I have learned so far from being run over:

I am blessed.
A nurse told me tonight, "you know David you are loved".
Do not put things off.
If I think of it. Do it.
Say I love you to those you love.
Call that person you had your eye on that you like.
Don't put it off... and talk to them.
If you have a good family your just damn lucky!
NEVER GIVE UP!
Fight for life! Hold on to it! It's worth it!

Thursday February 14 Day 48

HAPPY VALENTINES DAY!

8:55 am 6 pills. I broke down with doctor. I cried. I cried. I cried. I cried.
CRY CRY CRY CRY CRY
Why am I here still.
Why did I hold my blood back?
What am I going to do...
All I know that I can believe
Is I am loved.
More than I will ever know...
I need to paint...
Paint has been the only thing that has truly made sense.
I need paint on my hands.
I need paint on my hands.

I NEED PAINT ON MY HANDS!
I NEED PAINT ON THE SURFACE!
I NEED TO PAINT!
I NEED TO PAINT!

9:05 am - OT. Ow more sore feet. They hurt.

Gods and higher power I don't know what to do...
I can not return to CVS.
I miss my mom.
This accident is so much to bare; physical and mental. The physical will heal. The mental is being to handle everything no one but my self knows what I saw... So much to bare it feels as though this is all a dream... I should be dead! I should be in the ground. I am called a miracle. The doctors can not explain. Why I am here... They not only saved my life they brought me a new life.

This will help:

Concrete awareness; what can I touch, feel, see.
Say who you are.
Where you are.

My name is David.
It is Thursday.

I have tools to work through trauma.

Must stay in the now... right here right now just this...

Keep practicing and I can do anything!

2:30 pm Dad showed up. I know he is trying to be tuff around me. Controlling my emotions by not letting me cry around him. "I have control over everything". He says.

Where shall I begin? I am sure people will want to skim through to find the blood, gore, and horror that is real. No stunt double, no CGI, no smoke and wires.

My life has changed. My thinking has changed. My dreams changed. My relationship with my brother changed to where we now speak and have great conversations. This 'accident' I look at it as a blessing.

It brought faith, love, and courage to not give up. We all need a good story to help us make life a little easier. I have such a story.

9 PM is a challenge for me. That time triggers my awake time in ICU. Nightmares, sweats, waking and not falling back to sleep is common.

Honestly, this book I was told might be a journey to understand more about myself as an artist, a man, and someone just tying to live life. Scary it may be to face the ghosts and walk through and come out to the other side where ever that is.

In the brief moment as we drift off to sleep or when we wake. We ask ourselves questions perhaps out loud. I know I did. What is in store for me? What should I do next as an artist? Simple questions.
Some questions are answered. These questions are never answered in my time.

I try to live by some simple mantras. "Never give up!" Which is painted with stenciled 6-inch letters on the roof of my car. Right here, right now, just this. This one I admit is harder mostly because I let it.

Many questions were answered. Many things reinforced. Many questions raised. Beliefs reinforced.
Inner peace and light was never a question… I prayed and painted with the gods, spirits, and angels.

I felt the presents of the light many times in studio making art. I knew I was watched over and protected.

The accident tested many things; my faith in me, faith in my higher power, love just poured down on top of me... The amount of blood I lost I should never have kept my leg... I should never have LIVED! I should be dead! Yet, here I am writing a book about my experience, strength and hope!

Stanley Kubrick the film director said when he wrote beautiful mind "you need material to edit."

My good friend told me many times soon as you start writing that is when your book begins! So, I am writing! With Samuel a teddy bear that my friend mailed to me when I was on the rehab floor. Samuel is a small teddy bear that had many balloons. Samuel ate, slept, and went to rehab with me. He helped so much that no one knows! Samuel hung with me in my wheel chair riding shot gun. Yes, the bear slept a lot but he has protected me. When I go on the 'outside' he is still with me and sits on the restaurant table and smiles at everyone. Samuel waves at people too everyone smiles and waves back... The love of a simple teddy bear makes people smile.

Friday February 15, 2008 Day 49

Woke up many times. Too much noise even with ear plugs. 6am pills. 8am breakfast. Clean up. Got a few minutes before OT. Write in journal a few lines. Mood tired. I got my left leg some don't. So blessed it's over whelming to know gods work to have me do something! I was not meant to stay at CVS... Oh show me my job! Love I feel show me...

9:00 am - OT. The usual fine motor skill exercises.
10:00 am – PT. Leslie and I walked to elevators and down to the 3rd floor to see if Kelly my original occupational therapist had her baby.

12:00 – Lunch. A nurse had a t-shirt on: How can I miss you if you won't go away.

I miss my home group meetings.

Must tell my dad… the trauma is not over for me. It might be over for you… not for me!
My dad has never stayed in the hospital except for being born.

Sore left leg. Sore feet. Sore mind.

Tomorrow I leave at NOON.

I have been here so long…
I don't know what do…
Transition to outside world…

Bruce left today. I saw him wheel down the hall way to the elevators… he is going home! Before he left he pointed to his head… It's all in your head man. It's all in there… Take it easy he said… Bye Bruce.

I wheeled to my room… my day will be tomorrow.

Saturday February 16, 2008   Day 50

I am getting up. May be hard. I may hobble. I may fall… I will just have to get up. I died I saw the light. I don't know about anyone else. No one else knows what is going on in my head.

I got life and I am going to live it!

Sunday February 17, 2008   Day 51

First day home. I am blessed to have a good family. Ruff night. At 3 am I still could not sleep the pain was bad. I needed some liquid morphine for the pain so I could sleep. Finally, got to sleep. Woke up at 10 am. So far off regular hospital schedule. Today as I watched everyone. Run doing their own thing I truly began to cry. To think… if I did not save my life… one may be selfish and think of things like this. So close to death how many people would be affected. Now with 51 days I wonder what lies ahead. What mysteries, what love, what discoveries…

I see a bed side table filled with pill bottles none of which takes away my tears… Not tears of pain or love. I have a new life before me… It's overwhelming.

To sleep I take a diladid. Went off the methadone too soon with out being monitored and then released from hospital.

Slept from 8 pm to 4:30 am then woke at 6 am.

Monday February 18, 2008   Day 52

Woke at 8:30 am. Will now sign my art with days after. (1-50 in hospital) anything higher than 50 out of hospital.

Tuesday February 19, 2008   Day 53

9:00 am - Woke up. Slept well. Sleep is critical and in hospital and in hospital to much noise to sleep. Adjusting to routine of being on the outside. I manage to get a few hours of sleep at a time somehow.

For breakfast I had French toast with fresh strawberries. I remember I got 7 strawberries in the hospital every morning on my tray. I had befriended the dietitian… was honest with her I told her I could not eat anymore the regular diet… I had been in so long that I could not take it. Each bite I forced down my throat. Knowing full well it was better than going back on an IV or feeding tube. Knowing something about diet and knew I was not getting enough protein for healing. She got me the staff menu and I would order off that. The berries no one else got… She asked if I wanted them… some fiber and vitamin C and wonderful taste!

Alexander, my nephew was at school. Quiet. So, the quiet factor is increased… I miss my friends… wheeling the halls. Cracking jokes. Laughing. Crying. Alarms. Tubes. Tests. Pills. I still missed it all…

I moved on… "faked it" and did my screeches. Walked the neighborhood with the walker. Angry when the walker wheels stopped on the slightest bit of debris. I would pick up the walker and slam it down hard. My dad walking next to me would say, "calm be calm". I turned to him and said, my injury my healing… You have no idea what I am going through… David the trauma is in your head if you want it to be. After, that commit I know I can never expect him to understand or even try to understand. He is not capable of it. He does not he the tools a father might have to help his son through this. I will look for others for compassion and understanding… I know that it will be easier with help.

Every day I would get a little further down the street. I look back to where I was not long ago. With a tube down my throat and nose with no one thinking I would live. After the walking I would be wiped out and take a nap. Waking at noon in time to take my pills.

4 pm Just walked ¼ of the block. Phew second walk of the day. I have a shrink now for extra help with pstd. I can not hug anyone now with out crying so I am careful and not hug anyone.

Wednesday February 20, 2008   Day 54

Looked up my injury online. I knew the photos would be graphic and perhaps trigger trauma. The research gave me some understanding to my injury and helped me heal.
I am gaining more understanding moment by moment. For one I had to accept to that no one came to help me while I was bleeding to death on the sidewalk. No one held my hand. No one said, "help is on the way". Nothing. I was alone with my gods. I had to not have a resentment towards those people. Not one day has gone by where I think of the details several times a day. I think of the paramedics working on me. I do not recall extreme pain except for the moment of impact where the tire went over my leg. I remember saying OW! Real loud at the moment. Shock took over so no pain was felt. Still able to "talk and see" Images forever in my mind.

The doctors clamped off one end of the severed artery and sewed a Gore-Tex stint to both ends. Then let the blood go to test. A titanium rod was pounded into my femur. 30 or so stitches and staples sealed up the road mad of scares.

I figured out the time sequence since hit: once the call got out 3-5 minutes for the paramedics to get to me. 2 minutes for the artery to bleed out. 13 minutes in the helicopter. 4 ½ hours in surgery. These numbers run through my mind.

Sean Taylor of the Red skins was shot in the leg by someone robbing his home. No one thought it was a serious injury since it was in the leg. He died. I found more and more people who died with a severed femoral artery. Only found 3 people who lived. 2 guys shot in a war and a woman surfer. The first guy was in World War I his buddy used his boot laces for a tourniquet. The second guy was also shot. Both lost their legs. The woman surfer had the fin impale her leg 100 yards from shore. She managed to wrap the cord of her surf board around her leg and walk to shore screaming for help. She kept her leg.

I am on the list now of survivors.

Met with Dr. R my Psychotherapist today, he seems to be someone I can trust and that is what I need now.

Thursday February 21, 2008 Day 55

This "book" I am writing is taking shape. I decided to put it into a journal form. That way it can be picked up anywhere and be read. Plus, short compilations of thoughts, ideas, drawings, letters, what ever I decide to add.

Today: Dr. R, exercise, walk, visited fire station 1 the crew that saved me were not there. I just wanted to show them I had made it.

Titles of the book are on my mind.

What word, phrase, or book, can express what I am feeling…

I look up femoral artery again and the search becomes one gruesome story after another all ending in death.

Sometimes I wonder if my gods, angels, and spirits all put their hands on my bloody body and helped… The blood was under my left finger nails for a long time.
So, I know that I did something. It took many scrubbings to get the blood out. My first shower was over 2 weeks. I was sponged down in ICU once or twice. I did not care. Getting better came first.

I can still feel and hear the screams of patients in the night of ICU. In the morning the screaming stopped. Those people had died. I had a corner room and saw the nurses station in front of me and people slowly dying all around. Nurses would come to my room. I was one of the only few people out of the 18 that was able to talk. The nurses would come in and tell me that another motorcyclist came in… I could hear the screaming. He is hanging on the nurse said, he won't make it through the night… he just won't die. In the morning I did not hear anymore screaming. To me screaming meant life. When there was no screaming I saw priests and family members in front of the room. We will make arrangements. Crying. I just became numb… This place was the edge. Another bed would roll out and one would roll in. The sun rose and with it a new day. Eight days with a number 8 tube for the ventilator and nine days on the feeding tube. I gasped and gagged when I got the chance I would push that vent tube from side to side. My throat swelled. My hands were tied down for a few days case I rip out my tubes. Believe me when I had my hands untied to touch a letter board to communicate I wanted to yank the tubes out! Only a few sentences and my family would tie my hands down again. I could not speak. Not sedated. Staying in the same spot to wake to sleep. To dream. To mess my bed. The only chance to any peace was sleep. I was on drugs. That caused me to not go for 5 days and nights. I called for a bed pan one night. The nurse never came. She told me later a woman at the end of the ward coded. She made it. Messing my bed did not seem important anymore.

Thinking of the feeling is exulting the present is all that needs to be done.

Now that I am out… I think of things like showering in public at the YMCA with scars.

How to improve outlook.

I can use showering at the YMCA as an example: When I saw the backsides of all ages I realized that I could get wet and shuffle around these men. Sounds simple. When you take in account that I had to be bathed by a nurse. Huge leap.

NOON: Went for a walk around the housing development. Half a mile in 30 minutes with short brakes.

12:30 pm - Lunch. Sandwich.

2:00 pm - Psychotherapist.

The trickster is in my head again… not sure what is… the voices have come back. I heard them in the hospital. Now, they are back… Holding me! Fear. Uncertainly. My injured self is child.

All trauma is child- we want to cry.

I need to heal my own way not someone else's way.

I will be alright… just need to be patient and persistent.

Friday February 22, 2008 Day 56

Slept till 8 am – Breakfast = 2 eggs over easy, toast, milk.

Cried a lot before bed… a lot…. Cry for pain. Cry for surviving. Cry for release and to cleanse the wounds I have.

Lunch with dad: Mexican place- A little place only Mexicans eat at. Dad had some brown drink called Taharindo – It's fruit juice that tastes brown.

Lunch = beef burrito and enchiladas
Mexican food is medicine for the body and soul for me. Connects me with mother and culture. Connects with pleasure of senses.

Next stop. Visit Station 1 - the crew that saved me was not there. They showed us around the station- We were all little boys with big toys!

Beyond physical pain
Beyond physical pleasure
Beyond mental hardship
Beyond love of someone
Beyond god or gods
Beyond core of life…

I know from today response from station 1 is under 5 minutes. The whole thing was close. To close…

Feels as though I am here to do work and when I am ready I will do the work.

Being powerless over people, places, and situations, is something I must accept. In order to understand I am not in charge. I do not have control. When we sense or feel we have lost control anger, resentments, and perhaps a in pending doom folds upon us.

I did all I knew as an Eagle Scout to move my self out of harms way. I did that by moving out of the way of the last set of wheels headed towards me. May seem logical to just move. With bones sticking out, artery severed, and blood gushing I had no time to think I just moved. Sometimes we think of the "what if" their was no time to think or plan action just happened. Actually, I had no idea what had happened to my leg till much later.

Lying on the sidewalk I sized up the situation and thought of drawing a cool monster in the huge pool of blood by my head. I followed the blood to my shorts where the left side was drenched in blood. Reaching up I put my hand over the spot and put my head back down. Waited for help… Reading later, I found out that with this injury 2 minutes is all I had before dying.

People were at the seen watching. Watching me die… Alone.
To fight for my life.

When the paramedics arrived I heard them running up to me…
"BOY HE IS A MESS!"
"LOOK HE IS HOLDING HIS ARTERY!"

I knew time was running out… I had only seconds left to live.
Several IV's were started.
Extremely low on blood. They found no blood pressure.

Time was slipping… just living on the breaths of the gods…

Feeling my bowels empty I knew it was not long now… They
cut my shorts off my mangled body. Next, came my shirt… the
shirt my brother gave me that he did not want anymore… I loved
that shirt. "WE GOT TO DO IT NOW!" shouted a paramedic.
I could feel the neck brace go on… and just like we practiced in
Boy Scouts I was put on the back board… up and in the
ambulance the rush of oxygen inside gave me what I needed.

I remember the heads of the paramedics. Their helmets with
screen and the number 1 just like the movies… only now it was
not going to cut to commercial. This was no drama story… The
guy at my head asked my name over and over. I spelled it over
and over… "I DON'T KNOW WHAT HE IS SAYING! HE IS
BABBLING!"

Then I said the serenity prayer out loud… 'God grant me the
serenity to accept the things I can not change the power to
change…. I started over and just kept it up perhaps 2-3 times…
Then… Then… everything was gone. The ambulance was gone.
The paramedics were gone and their shouting. My shouting was
gone. Everything was replaced by a vast white light. Calm.
Peaceful. Restful. Beautiful. It lasted a few moments. Long
enough to know what it was. Then that was gone. Then there
was nothing. Nothing at all…

I learned in life and creating art never to give up! There is always a solution. Asking others for their view on things then I would take all that and make my own decision.
Sleeping on things gives the mind a rest and in the morning refreshed ready to carry on.
The answers do come. Sometimes the answers come when I am making art. The simple painting to the viewer may have been a struggle. To have everything come together and create something worthy for me often just happens. When I get in the way is when nothing is produced. I believe only with the gods that I can really do any art at all.

The paper and paint lay waiting… the brush knows.

I am here to just hold the medium and put medium to surface.

What does this have to do with what happened to me? Plenty. It is the art that will help me heal my mind… Only by writing and drawing I am I able to continue on and handle the post trauma stress disorder.

Art prevails
Art can not die
Art is in us all no matter if it comes out or not

Saturday February 23, 2008   Day 57

8:41 am – No pain. Woke up 1-2 times during the night.

Feeling rested and well!
I feel GREAT!
I FEEL GREAT!
Walked into the main room and saw Alexander playing. I stole two kisses on top of the head of my nephew even though the little guy is still sick and coughing.

BIG BREAKFAST- Omelet, potatoes, fresh orange, 1 boost (yuck!), o.j., 2 pieces of toast with jam.

11 am - Still feeling good! Did stretching exercises. Made some calls. So far so good. No snags. I must remember the good days.

Found a photo Christine took of me 3 days after accident. My wrists are tied down, vent and tubes every where, my eyes swollen and red, fingers like sausages. Fat fat fat fingers! Ha ha!

Feels good looking at the photos- I have come a long way in a short amount of time!

11:06 am- GREAT DAY! Golden moment. Strong enough.

Went to the park walked bare foot! The park had a rubberized flooring. Felt great to walk with out shoes or walker!

2:00 pm – went for ice cream.

3:00 pm – Crashed and went to bed.

8:00 pm – woke up. I was in pain. Hard to move. I yelled for my dad. No answer. In fact the more I yelled I could hear the TV. get louder.

I knew I had to somehow get out of bed to get help. I managed to get half way through the main room and saw my dad on his laptop watching boat videos. "Oh your hungry?! I am stuffed he said." "I thought you were stuffed." Oh I was pissed! I was screaming your name! I told him, "I hope I can hear you over the TV. when I take care of you."

I fixed something simple and quick to just shove down my throat. Dad never did get up from his laptop. The help line is over. Accept it and move on.

8:20 pm – called Jennifer she was home and I spoke to her till 9:30.

God's plan not mine. I am a handful as an artist. Relying on gods, spirits, and angels. That's who I pray and meditate to for so many years now.

That faithful day was a day full of faith. I reborn not by gods but into another level of being and understanding few know about. Book or no book writing is in me and coming out! My entire wiring has been ripped out and replaced!

I just rolled over on my stomach with left leg bent up. First time in 2 months been on my stomach. So hard on the knee I turn over again.
As hard as it is for me to continue on at times... I find the strength. This story must and will be told.

Sunday February 24, 2008 Day 58

Woke at 10 am. Dad is so focused on girlfriend coming to visit. That's all he thinks about. On the phone he tells her he can't sleep. I laugh and think of all the countless lost nights of sleep with alarms, tubes, screams, and everything else. May be selfish to think. Of my self like this... I know what is coming. He will be gone and stay at a hotel soon as she shows up. I can not count on him to get me to doctors offices or anything else.

For pain he gave me what looked like my sleeping pills. "Watch what your giving me" I told him. Turns out it was the right stuff. He gave me morphine and ms contin.

To have 14 years sobriety and then to be on morphine and other pain killers for months. It has worn me down...

finished through the bottle of Dilaudid as directed.

I can tell you morphine is junk. Pure and lovely for pain. Oh it is great for pain. My mom was on it the last days of her life. It is junk and fills your mind with beautiful illusions and then gouges out your eyes and lies to you! Pure and ugly turning on you. Honestly, I like morphine and had to come off it twice during this accident. I can not tell you to take it. Please do not take it! I had a reason… a very large reason. A semi truck of a reason.

As an artist living among non artists I feel more different. The Gore-Tex stint, rod in my leg, and trauma in my mind. The whole experience just raised the bar. Been trying to live through… How I manage? Coping? At times I don't and that is when I have to accept where I am and get into action. It is action that I manage and get through.

Some coping skills I have learned that work for me:

1. Call someone: I have a group of people I call for what I call direct method. To talk to someone else; I have started off crying and in 10 minutes I am laughing. Share my experience and in process helps the other person.

2. Write: Writing put the thought, feeling, emotion, or idea down on paper so you and others can read it. Intend to not hold back in writing. To hold back can be dangerous. I must be free to write about any and all subjects. Accounts of the accident, what goes on inside my head, relationships with other people, my feelings I must an do talk about freely of drugs- no one in my family understands.

As a sober person managing pain with medication is something I need to write about. I don't need anyone tell me I am not sober taking these drugs. When a truck runs you over and you wake up in a hospital alive morphine becomes your friend and you rely on that friend to make you feel good. That friend though will turn on you and show you horror of horror. Nothing will stop you from getting "MORE"

For someone who is not an addict or alcoholic they see it as every 3 to 6 hours or as prescribed by a doctor. Not all at once. They don't understand and that is o.k.

For now my recovery comes in waves. I feel "GREAT" now. Tomorrow or the next I may feel impending doom flood me.

Doom. Nobody knows this doom unless a person has been "there". No words can express my doom. Just that it feels as though it will always be there... and that is not true. Doom does go away. It may not feel as though it will... It will.

OUT OF THE DANGER ZONE

Everyone marvels at the miracle of a near death experience, but fewer people 'check up' on me now. My head is still filled with trauma, though. My body filled with drugs. People are people. They see no danger. Samuel my teddy bear, or "transitional object" according to medical terminology, knows all I say. He tells no one. He has ears but no mouth.

WHEN AN ARTIST DIES

When an artist dies that you love, their art you love, the process you love, the reaction you love to show that you love that the art is sold. When that artist who died is yourself.... You learn rather quickly that nothing is the same. Sure, the people around me see the same old David plus a bunch of physical scars. They only know what they can see. They cannot understand what they cannot see—and that is what is in the artist's mind. And they never will understand. That's okay, though.... It was my first time dying.

COMING BACK TO LIFE – Journaled

My first time writing about coming back to life.
My first time surviving.
Nothing matters now that mattered before.

My thinking,
My processing,
My understanding,
Gone –

When my walker stopped on another shell again, I picked up my walker and slammed it down.

My father said, "Calm. Be calm."

I turned to him. "It's not your injury. It's not your recovery."
He was trying to control my feelings, but I was living my feelings. He feels as though he can control everything, but he can control nothing.

People tell me to smile.
People tell me to be happy.
People tell me….

None of the people who tell me these things have been crushed and just watched as they bled to death.

But I must not fault anyone.
I must not.
They have not experienced.

I feel I have a singleness of purpose for this world.

I don't think like you.
I don't want to think like you want me to think.
I don't act like you want me to act.

If I did….
I would be buried and have tears and flowers on my grave.

WHAT SAVED ME? – Journaled

I did not think.
I instantly acted on instinct.
There was no time for anything else.
Blood was everywhere…. Everywhere.
I did not have a 'buddy.' This was no war.
I was on my own but with many gods and angels….
People just watched as they dialed on their cell phones.
I wonder if they took pictures.

I cannot dwell on the the 'ifs.' It is fruitless to do so….

The only thing I can focus on is the here and now.

Progress is progress. It may be crappy at times, but it is still progress.

Lying in bed, I listened to my dad and his girlfriend make dinner for the rest of us. Dad was putting on a great show by overacting and being giddy that his girlfriend was with him. Alexander was playing and screaming! No matter what the adults did, they could not quiet that child. The screaming was loud, even from my room with the door shut. Then I remembered that every situation has many sides to look at. Alexander reminded me of the patients screaming in the ICU unit of the hospital. As long as they screamed, they were still alive! When the patients stopped screaming, I knew the priest would come shortly after.

Scream = Life.
No scream = No life.

It is all about perception and how you choose to look at things.

Monday February 25, 2008 Day 59

7:30 am - Dad called and woke me up. Going to take me to rehab therapy.

8:00 am - Cooked and ate eggs. Back to bed.
8:30 am - Got dressed and got back into bed.

Dad came in the house and saw me still in bed. He was very angry, yelling he said, "your not ready! I am out of here!" I tell him I am ready. Dad yells back, "YOUR NOT READY! BYE!" I whipped off the blankets and got up telling him over and over I am ready. I am ready. He was not happy he had to drive me to rehab. His girlfriend sat in the back seat. Silence the entire ride. Boy was he mad!

Dad just seemed put out he had to drive his son when he could be with his girlfriend. I felt like a box of Florida oranges. Dumped off at rehab with out a word. The car sped away...

Later, I had a meeting with my psychotherapist. In the session, I told him I never have been rolled over by a semi truck before. "I don't know how to act" Happy? I am told to be HAPPY! Dad's girlfriend tells me to smile. I tell her I can do what I want where I want when I want.
I really am just going to write it all...

Tuesday February 26, 2008 Day 60

Yes, today is day 60. Just a number. Another day making my own breakfast. Called dad no answer off with girlfriend. Did not even leave message.

Christine came home and we talked about our weekends. Insurance problems were dealt with today. Forms, faxes, money, phone calls. That was my day.

A collector called me to see new works. I told them I was in an accident and had nothing new to show them I would call them when there was something to show them.

Walked out side to pool side where papers and paint were setup.
Scratched around with some yellow paint. Just to do something
rather than nothing. The feeling was empty so I left the paint
dry.

Creepy. I have been taking my mom's old pain pills. Christine
kept them from when mom was sick. Gave the pills to me for a
temporary solution until we can see the doctor at the rehab for
new meds.

9:01 pm – Called Ruth to help walk me through my pill taking.
I am on my own with this. I don't want to be in charge of
morphine tablets and having liquid morphine on my night stand.
Creepy. I don't trust my self with drugs.

Ruth told me to breathe. Are you eating enough protein. No,
dad is off with girlfriend. Physical challenge to stand long
enough to cook something. 60 days after the accident the mental
part leaves me confused, frustrated, and angry.

Kindness creeps in somehow and says, "GIVE YOUR SELF
SOME SLACK!" "HOW MANY PEOPLE DO YOU KNOW
WHO SURVIVED THIS AND HAVE YOUR LEG!" I found
only one woman named Heather who is a surfer who saved
herself.

I lie here now with tears dried on my face. The salt. The
sorrow. Words become dried and scatter… The gods know.

Healing. Healing of limbs. Healing of mind? Perhaps the doctors can breach me to a point to "cope" – after that what do you say to someone who has died? Stay in the moment? Sure. One day at a time. One hour at a time. I don't want pity. I just want after all this… after all the rods, grafts, vents, tubes, ventilator, contusions that covered my body. I just want a hug! A long full filling hug. The tubes always got in the way. When the tubes were all out I would hug nurses more than my own family. We could cry all we wanted to in the arms of a nurse. This was not the case of my own family especially my dad who told me not to cry when I hugged him. I decided to not hug my family anymore.

Today, dad and his girlfriend fly back home.

My lifeboat is at home. Countless friends have offered to help me when I come back. I have no desire to drive a car for a long time.

What makes me happy:

1. Being able to breathe on my own.
2. Going to the toilet on my own.
3. Having my entire left leg which I kiss saying thank you.
4. Loved by the gods, spirits, and angels. I am closer to them now.
5. Loved by many people

Wednesday February 27, 2008 Day 61

8:30 am - Woke up. Slept great. Out of bed at 9 motivation to get up? Need to eat something to take pain medications. Dislike depending on drugs so I can function. It's what needs to be done. The morning tasks of getting dressed and bathroom run had to be broken into many smaller tasks. Had to physic my self up to do these things.

7:08 pm – I have no mother to go home to. Talking to my friends who I think of mother figures comforts me. They all say, "I wish I knew what to say to you." Sobbing I would tell them being present right now is a huge help. Being present on the phone does not seem enough they would say. The woman told me, "I wish I was there with you". Sobbing was all the other person heard for a while.

Sleep. Sleep is needed for healing.

My theme Song. By Queen:

I like to ride my bicycle
Bicycle
Bicycle

To begin this story is a journey.

No one dares to think about, dream, or even saying the word is hard.

This story has more blood then most people will see in their lives.

I have read without fear there can be no courage.

I have a story to tell. Medical professionals read the title of my medical chart. They gasp and put their hands over their mouth and close their eyes. Some have reached over and squeezed my hand. Some read the chart out loud. Then look at me standing. Then they hit the second notebook. Looking up they say... you have a story to tell. You must tell keep on telling it.
So I do done now do tells it... can you tell a bit of the south is warring off on me.

I tell Bill and Jeff the rehab transport drivers my story. The message of life, blood, reacting, taking nothing for granted. Live in the moment.

I tell people when I was loaded into the ambulance that I prayed out loud. Steven the paramedic at my head talked to me. I will never forget that guys helmet.

God grant me the serenity to accept the things I can not change
The courage to change the things I can and the wisdom to know the difference.

Thursday February 28, 2008   Day 62

In PT today the therapist Kristy said, "I am going to hurt you!"

Oh I said, "as if the truck tire didn't hurt". I winced, eyes bulged and when she was done. I walked! With out any aid. Kristy jumped up and down. She moved me on to the parallel bars where I walked back and forth a few times. I was handed a cane and told to walk around the gym.

We passed by a circle of wheel chairs tossing a large beach ball. It missed someone's hands and wacked Kristy in the head. I was so focused on walking I missed the whole thing. Kristy said, "I just took a header for you you'd probably topple over"!

Friday February 29, 2008   Day 63

MY FEET ARE HAMBURGER

Today is the day when it is all right for girls to ask the boys to marry them. It is called Sadie Hawkins day. Sadie was a character in the old L'il Abner cartoons and could never get asked out so always did the asking. Noon met with hey another doctor! This time to get new prescriptions. Oh what a relief to be off of morphine again.

1 pm - can you guess? Yup a doctors visit.
2 pm - cell phone trouble. More money.
3 pm - Christine picked me up from doctors. Stopped for a burrito oh my was it good!

Next stop GNC for protein shakes. Christine knew the owner and we walked around scanning the pictures and posters of the body builder's poses. I bellied up to the counter. The owner asked what I wanted in my smoothie. Peanut butter and chocolate plus what ever you want. Just wing it! Then I told him the story… His eyes bugged out and leaned over the counter and looked at me standing. MAN YOU MADE IT! WOAH! Yeah, I said, I don't give up! The owner and body builder who has won completions shook his head like so many others. He handed over a quart sized smoothie! WOW! THE TASTE WAS FANTASTIC AND LOADED WITH PROTEIN! Next stop the gym. Christine worked out with her personal trainer as I watched and sucked down the smoothie. She introduced me to the usual people working out. Some already knew of my story and when they saw me they could not believe I was walking around so well. A small crowd circled me as I told others the story. The usual silence and gasps followed by a range of questions. "how did you know what to do"? "did I loose any weight"?

An Indian guy looked at me… you saw the light, he said. Yes, I did. I told him. I looked at him… He knew my language. You saw the light. I asked him. He said, yes I have. The language we spoke transcended past all in the room and we both knew. You must continue to tell your story to people. Never stop telling your story. The world needs to hear… He smiled and walked away. We knew death. All the texts of the ages speak of death. There is nothing to it. Death is death. I can continue with language that only a few speak. You will know how to die when the time comes.

All of the people gathered around said they were inspired and uplifted. Never give up! I told them and smiled. We can do anything! Several people said, "you should do this for a living"! The world needs to hear you!

Few people survive this type of injury. Only a few have both legs! Should I use my miracle to make money? With great love from the gods, spirits, and angels, comes great responsibility!

To home. To sleep. We then went to Out Back Steak house. To, shall we say protein up! We were the only skinny table in the place.

That night I used a trick my psychotherapist recommended for sleep. The repeating nightmares had returned. I would have one. Wake up sweating and terrified to sleep again. Reason being when I fell back asleep I would have the same nightmare over again. This is my repeating nightmare. This night I sat up in bed shook my fist in the air and cursed out loud directing my curses to the night mares! "GO THE F AWAY! LEAVE! I DON'T NEED YOU! GO!" The voices came back in my head… We are not leaving! We own you! I repeated my curses and shaking my fist! The voices went away. Quiet lowered into my room. That night I had no nightmares. The next night I repeated my chants and curses! No nightmares that night as well. Repeating this for many nights. Each night free of nightmares.

Saturday March 1, 2008 Day 64

When we admit defeat there is now where to go but up! I am scared. I feel alone. Post trauma stress disorder for me is sneaky and patient. Running the accident over and over in my mind is a way to control what happened. The crying comes and goes. The anxiety, fear, frustration, depression all comes and goes. Accept it and learn to live with it. I am told by others who have ptsd that it will get better. I am also told it will come back. Having a great day with all the joys of life only that night to have sweats and nightmares.

I am clear of the soul of the inner world – the gods. There is a place for my wondering soul. I have found my personal legend. I have found love.

Sitting on a couch at the YMCA a gentleman asks me... Are you a speaker? Your voice has power and intriguing qualities. I have been in the TV. and film industry for over 20 years I know a voice when I hear it!

I then proceeded to tell "the story". His eyes fixated and smiled. Your story must be told to a large group! He said.

I did not press his career I saw that he knew of the language I spoke of...

Sure enough! He spoke of a motor cycle accident when he was in his twenties. Right after he was hit he got up on his feet and looked down to the circle of blood beneath him. He then sat back down... His left foot had been moved 180 degrees so the toes faced behind him! His leg was such that the doctors did not know how to fix it. It was severally managed. This was before the use of pins. They decided to cast the leg for fear of infection. For 8 months his leg was in a cast. Three times the doctors came to him and said... we have to cut your leg off there is nothing we can do for it. The man refused each time. Find a way to keep my leg the man said. I will not have you cut my leg off! The man ended up keeping his leg. The doctors became specialist after working on this man. The man never gave up and the doctors learned a new language.

The man smiled and moved his leg saying I never let the doctors cut my leg off.

The man next to him was silent the whole time through out our stories. When we were through he got up with a stunned look in his eyes and smiled at both of us and blessed us both. He knew not what to say. When he did speak he knew the two of us traveled few ever go and came back – and said, "I am in honor of hearing you both speak"... He then walked away.

We all have our own personal trucks in our lives. My truck did not stop me it just slowed me down.

Your truck may come in all sorts of shapes and sizes. You may want to lose weight, ask that person out on a date, that book you want to write, that trip you want to take. You know your truck… it is slowing you down.

I think of my truck as a blessing.

My brother and I are talking and emailing on a regular basis. Before the accident we would say hi maybe. Turns out we are a lot a like.

No matter how much of the body you have or don't have. Your personal legend can be achieved. It will be achieved. You move your mind and body forwards you can do it. The mountain is only so high to climb, the race distance does not change once you start, losing weight is no more than you need to lose.

MY SISTER

At the age of forty-five, my sister had her first child. At such an age, she was at risk to have children. When she was twenty-eight weeks, something happened, and she had to deliver or she and her son would die. Nothing stood in the way of her having that child, though! She achieved her goal.

We went to visit mother and child in the hospital. A sixth sense spoke to me and let me know my sister would thrive and excel! Baby Alexander was in the preemie unit. Only two people at a time were allowed go into his room. My eyes rested on a baby who was no bigger than my hand. He was covered in tubes and monitoring devices. The room was very sensitive. A monitor showed a one or two degree increase as we walked in.

That sixth sense spoke to me again—this boy would thrive and bring joy! Indeed, two months later, Alexander left the hospital, bringing joy to our family.

After Alexander's birth, my sister gained sixty pounds. She did not become clouded by the what happened to her size and weight. She turned it into an example for others and made the goal to be fit. She formulated a plan and lost all of the weight. She even created a program and put it on a DVD to share with the whole world.

How did she create her DVD? She knew what she wanted to say and spoke in a language people would understand—simple and clear. The setting of her recording was a home that was in the family. With what she knew from her personal goal achieved, she shared the steps she took.

She never gave up on this huge undertaking. The DVD had to be a certain length—no more, no less. She hired a local production company that was family-run. She managed to keep costs down and be resourceful while still keeping her personal goal in mind. She finished what she started out to do, taking an idea and adding to it until it was complete.

My other sister, while she was in college, used to sit and watch T.V. a lot. She liked to order pizza. When the pizza man came to deliver, she would yell at him to come in. The guy would come in, pick her wallet up off the table, and hand it to her to be paid. Needless to say, she became a little round.

Then, she began running. She started eating better foods and lost the weight. Soon, she was sponsored by Nike. How did she do it? She got a pair of shoes and had a personal goal to not be round anymore.

Now she's in the masters group (those over forty years old), with several marathons under her belt. She even ran in the Olympic marathon trials. In her first triathlon, she placed second and did not even know it until she crossed the finish line.

She tells me there are triathlons for everyone! There is one for swimmers in a pool, and there is one for people who just walk.

Seventy percent of Americans are overweight, and, because of their excess weight, many of them have health issues in their prime instead of later in life. I saw plenty of overweight people in the hospital rehab complain about the pain they were in after they had their knees replaced. But if you have to take two or three hundred pounds through the normal paces of a day without regular exercise or a healthy diet, it doesn't take long before you need to have your knees replaced.

My mother had a friend who had been overweight for as long as I could remember. Her doctor told her lose the weight or risk a future with diabetes and insulin shots. She 'chose' to lose the weight, and she did. She lost over 50 pounds, and, more importantly, she kept it off! It was not hard. She just changed her diet and walked. That was it.

Wednesday March 19, 2008

Woke up slept badly- ah used to it- will just get so physically tired I will pass out like before-

Leg was so much in pain and sore and man if there was something in reach I would have... it was... Damn I am trying so hard to be in moment. Focus. I got to sitting position. I knew my body I had to move! swung the legs over and somehow made it to the bathroom. Dam the drugs! POOPS suck on pain meds. Ah I stink! Hunched over in pain and my mind just a fuzzy mess. I stand up again. The toilet is regular height yet it is so painful to sit cus' the leg gets pitched and nerves. the hospital toilet are at wheel chair level. OK turn water on for shower... will help with pain/soreness. Just stand there with all hot water streaming down my twisted body. Soap. Need soap. least I will be clean and in pain. ha ha!

Stepping out- slowly- can't afford to fall now! dry off- grab a yogurt and go back to bed. only up for 1/2 hr. feels like the whole day. Rest. Write. phone calls. breathe. breathe! Please tell me it will get better.... lie to me some more tell me it will get better... tell me something. phone rings.... david you still do not have coverage.....

Grab the phone and have my redrum hands ready to do battle! bloody sod!

I am told that I am reinstated by HR! I have a job - and coverage... only thing is the computer has to catch up to the rest of the world. Pending. pending take days... I don't have days. Fax the stuff to the surgery center... Meanwhile, $502.10 is the number the surgery center wants... we are working towards to avoid to pay cus' the pending insurance.

Tell me something... when the doctors asked me if I meant to get crushed by the truck if my answer was YES! I probably would be in a locked down ward. At least I would not have to deal with this paper work mess. I would be putting jigsaw puzzles together again and painting with ketchup and mustard.
Now I just have live on life's terms with all the bs and the trauma as well...

I watched a movie the other night and the actor turned on a table saw and was going to rip a piece of wood.... I KNEW THAT HE WAS GOING TO... damn the blood was all over the place and they put him on a chopper.... I watched this on my laptop with ear plugs. I lost it! crying. ripped the plugs from my ears and covered my face.

NEVER WILL I GIVE THE BASTARDS THE GLORY! THIS IS MY VICTORY I SHALL BEAT THIS AND GO ON! old Winnie was right NEVER GIVE UP!

NEED FOOD! off to PT soon. more later.

Day 53

Life. Family. Home. Food. Clothing. Shelter. Love. Phew. My experience of the accident only a few have 'been there' to know.

The direction of this book is something unknown to me. I am surely not the same person now.

I feel as though my thinking is compared to the jigsaw puzzle boxes I opened in occupational therapy.

Without doing many puzzles in the past I First started with 100 piece puzzles. These puzzles were done in about twenty minutes. The Therapist then gave me 1,000 piece puzzle thinking it would take me a while to do. The image reminded me of a painting Grandma Mosses would have painted.

First, I separated the edge pieces and quickly formed the border. Defining the space of the image. I then separated the pieces with similar colors. The puzzle took shape and went together.

Now take the idea of the puzzle and there is no border to define the image. In fact the image is infinite in my mind.

Some believe in 'thinking outside the box'. I used to say before the accident I cut the box up and put it in the recycle bin.

Now, there is not only no box. There is no limit to my thinking. Perhaps it was always there and just needed a HUGE TRAUMA to jar it loose!

In writing this 'book' may be a form of therapy to work through and to ease my trauma still running in my mind.

Day 54   Wednesday February 20

I searched the Internet today on my type of injury and found that the bled to death time is two minutes.

Puts everything into place… or makes things not such….
Such…. A big deal. What can be done in two minutes? Name some things. GO! Not much right. Also, heard my dad say that my older sister told him we might lose Dave…. Ok so I did not die I beat all the possible odds. Even the doctors all asked me how I did it? What did you know what to do? I did not have much of an answer. My best guess is that I intuitively knew how to handle the situation when it arrived.

Tuesday February 26, 2008   Day 60

Phew. That word sums up today. I woke up and made breakfast consisting of two eggs, toast, milk, and orange juice. I called my attorney. I love their office soon as they answer they say hi David. It is a small office and they say "don't worry get better and we will take care of it!" It sure makes life easy with a good attorney.

Dad came at 12:15 to take me to physical therapy. I cannot make the ride exciting his girlfriend Anne rode in the back. Nothing was said the entire way. I just feel like a crate of oranges being transported and once dropped off they took off. Dad is in the mist of dating again after some fifty years. From what I gather he did not date a whole lot. It is good to see him happy.

I never have been hit by a semi before - so I don't know how to act...

sounds like a fucking cop out right?! well I am not the same person.

today was hard and I am waiting till 9pm to call some people....

just seems my family is cutting the lines and I am on my own.

scared- cus' I don't know anyone down here in Florida-

yeah I should go to a meeting- one of the calls at 9pm

the only thing that I can say is I know I am not alone! I did not die for a reason even though it may seem like I should have just let the blood flow... yet I am here typing alive and breathing...

death is beautiful.

knowing that and living I must tell people so I know that I must continue on this journey.

Wednesday February 27, 2008 Day 61

For the first time in some time I struggled to leave bed this morning. I had no direction or purpose other than to proceed on. My mind was stead fast on over burden with 'the day'. It was nearing 9 am the pain meds would soon ware off and it would be even harder to 'proceed'. I took small baby steps. Swung the sheets and blankets off my body. The cold air hit and only movement to putting on socks and other clothing in order to be warm. Then off to the bath to endure pain. Being on pain meds stops your bawls and creates painful experience. Washing of hands and face. By now my feet are telling me hey buddy we cannot do our job much longer we need to move! My mind swimming, dancing, and racing all in the name of trauma. What next? To the kitchen. Fill your hole and take meds. By now it is 9:30 am and I am wiped out! Line down. Yes, the phone rings never when your vertical. More medical jingle jangle that makes me want to... Anger I cannot afford to be I need rest. I just say ah "it's ok!" what the hell they gonna do to me? Kill me? Ha! Been there done that! Poor guy from the insurance company. I told him "I should have just died!" "It would be less paper work and I would not have to sign any of it!"

It sure is good to have an excellent attorney that says, "just get better we will handle it." Phew, I laid back in bed and got some rest. When yet again the phone goes off. The details matter little at this point. All I can say is some people need to grow up! Not be so wrapped up in their micro cosmos and be a responsible adult.

The truck just did not run over my femur and for those who have no idea what that part of the body is. Look it up. The truck ran over my sisters, brother, father, all their friends, my friends, people I do not even know! All of which I got mail, phone calls, and e-mails. The horror it brought in an instant!

I do not want pity. Most everyone is speechless and say "I don't know what to say to you?" I tell them, "hey I never have been through this before and neither have you."

The fact you made an EFFORT to call me. That you are here now speaking to me means a lot. Most times I say this to the person I am crying I realize how close I was to death. Any closer and I would still be dead. I see what REALLY matters what really counts. Love. Friendship. Trust. Belief.

Christine came home early today we went out and buzzed round. Had Mexican food out.

Mom's death was drawn out for two years each day closer to her death.

yup- I saw it on feb 1

check out this site-
http://www.woostercollective.com/

street art from around the world.

actually I am growing tired of this site
but it is fun cus' it is a blog type
that involves all medium.

managing my pain is hard on my own-
so used to nurses like you asking every few hours
what number... now I take 7 or so meds on my own.

I got my dad to take the liquid morphine off my
night stand... yes I have thoughts of using morphine
and drinking... mostly drugs. I cannot GLORIFY DRUGS!

ok--- so my scocolalist (sp.) or shrink esp in PTSD
he says it is early for me to have it... right now he
says I have extreme trauma in my head since I saw everything
this does not help... I took notes and he says "YOU ARE
DOING EVERYTHING RIGHT!" this is much harder than
stopping drinking!
he is a great guy I feel safe with him.

My dad drove me to the station no. 1 who saved my life.

the head guy was not in-- they did not seem to thrilled to see me...
my dad just told me after dinner he noticed this to... and that the reason he thinks is that the EMT's see a lot of people dead.

I have searched my injury and have yet to find ONE person who lived!
I cried myself to sleep cus of this information... I finally said... I survived... I am here...

the EMT said we respond to seen under 5 minutes.
bleed to death from this artery is 2 minutes...

for all counts I should be dead

yet I am typing you this email

I should be HAPPY AND REJOICE people tell me...

yet I am depressed and reliving the event over and over...

I actually felt shame and embarrassed using a walker to walk up to the station 1
to see the EMT unit...

ok so the Dilaudid pain med just kicked in and I can handle the pain.

I had an idea for the community of Berwyn before the accident.

I want to form a arts community center. for all the arts/dance/acting/etc.
where we can hear music-and every thing. Berwyn is RICH with art and music.

this idea is very similar to the morphine trips I had...

a safe place where art can be made and shown...

also- I have a 'PLAN FOR THE BOOK'

To put it in journal form and short entries- with art/photos.
leading up to me running 1 mile with my sisters. 1 mile= 5280 feet
so far I can walk 1/2 mile with a walker.

56 days ago I had a vent in and was fighting to live.

today I am understanding to survive this injury is rare.
it saddens me that people died while I am here...

I must go on as painful physically and mentally---
I must rest.
I must give myself time.

I feel much better after writing

I died... and came back. I don't question why me? Only I have work to do when called upon. Death is beautiful. The living will know how to die when the time comes.

Monday March 10, 2008

Woke up crying. Pain. Crying not from pain just crying... Had to PEE BAD! What motivates me? A great motivator for me is having to PEE AND POOP! That sets to be priority number one! Or two.

Move out of bed or I will mess it.

The pain and tightness creates doom!
Doom!
Pain!
Pills take pain and wraps it up and smothers it.
Sadness lingers.

Crying over breakfast. The tears just won't stop! Need to feel emotions. When emotions take over not allowing you to function your life then it becomes a problem. Non stop crying for an hour is a problem especially when I don't know "why" I am crying. I begin writing an email to someone that may help… No I need to call someone now! I call Robert. "Hello, Dave. Oh good you got a moment? I am…" All Robert hears is my crying. Oh my I thought I was bad? He says. What's going on!? I am unable to speak. All I can do is sob into the phone. Several minutes go by before I can talk. Somehow I manage through the sobbing and choking of tears to put some words out. I don't know… I feel doomed!

Robert is the man who knows what I speak of… He has been through a ton of life. He knows pain all to well. He listens to me. That's what I need. He was so happy to hear from me. He thought he was having a ruff day until I called. Just by calling him he felt better. Life is easy when we ask for help. I can not be a victim if I am in control.

The crying stopped. In less than 15 minutes I am laughing at some wild crazy story that Robert had just experienced. Laughing! Right action leads to right thinking. A phone call away is countless people for me to get through what ever life throws me. Does this make me weak? No way! It works both ways. The receiving caller experiences being needed and has a chance to help. When they need help they know I am there for them.

Wednesday March 12, 2008

Went to the orthopedic surgeon today for my knee pain. The x-rays showed 2 screws in my hip and 2 screws in my knee. My sister Christine or I or anyone else in the family did not know I even had screws there! The surgeon put his finger right on the screw head….

BAM! I screamed! The head of the screw was causing inflammation and pain. It did not cause pain until I really began walking a lot. In the hospital I was in a wheel chair most of the time or in bed. I only walked a couple hundred feet for physical therapy.

So, the joke now is I got screwed and did not even know it. This should take the pain away.

I have not slept well at all the last few nights; sweats, nightmares, restless. The usual traumas run of the mill stuff.

Yesterday and today I got a big package in side about 200 cards of mail art. Here is the letter from the elementary school teacher sent me.

Dear David,

Glad our MAIL ART worked! (Your brilliant idea)
OK, here's the story as to how this happened:
Two years ago I received a great postcard called MAIL ART- Make art, It's fun!

Not knowing who sent it and being an over protector of kids (mother and teacher), I didn't act on it, but I did keep the card. When I was talking with a 4th grade class about local artists one of the students said, "he lived next door to a local artist." He said the artist had a web-site. I asked him to bring in the address and we could see if the local artist, David Gerbstadt, would like to talk about being an artist. The next week he brought in one of your great t-shirts w/your website on the back. I recognized the artwork and showed the class your postcard. (The really amazing thing is that I could actually find it!) As I was going to e-mail you to ask if you could give us a few minutes on "life as an artist", he told me about your accident. SO.....YOUR MAIL ART idea came to mind. The kids (each and every class) had a great time creating MAIL ART esp. because they knew you would love it.

But the story doesn't end there. I was telling one of my wonderful friends who teachers art at an alternative school about our MAIL ART reach out.

Heal!

Suzanne

March 13, 2008

1:48 AM: I was able to sleep a couple hours then I woke up and can not go back to sleep. I don't question when it happens now. It just is. Gives me time to write. Thinking after waking only has people renting space in my head. The meeting with Dr. Ray who is my psychologist comes to mind. He told me there has never been any studies about dream analysis while on morphine. Seems like a wide open cookie jar of a chance to do some wild study. I could go on pages of dribble about morphine and how it is to be on it. It is used only in sever trauma cases and for pain when someone is dying. My mom was on morphine in her final days of cancer.

To those of you who wonder to try morphine "just for fun" or are using drugs and have already tried it. Now is a good a time as any to get help with your drug use. Nothing to be ashamed of. I had to work through using morphine and was weaned off of it twice during this accident. I talked to friends and wrote a lot. I got through. It was not an easy thing to come down off morphine. Nights with horrible recurring nightmares, not being able to sleep, and sweating. I wanted to give in many times and go back to using not to take the pain use so I did not hurt so bad.

I wonder now that I am out of hospital and finishing with out patient rehab about; having a girlfriend, living on my own again, and working. My idea of a relationship with a woman seems foreign to me. My wants, desires, and ideas have changed. Scars I am told are "macho!" I sure hope so. Recently, I asked someone out and they were flattered I asked them but they said no.

They gave me a reason why they did not want to date me. I feel… I feel broken. My mind feels broken. My spirit is strong. My sense of what I believe in is extremely closer.

Woman do not want a broken mind in a relationship. I know I must stay positive and somewhere there is someone waiting who has compassion, love, respect, warmth, and wants to walk through time with me.

10:10 AM Was able to finally get some sleep. Resting in bed with a congested head.

3:30 PM Physical rehab was great. Improved over scores and walked outside with therapist. I joked around how when I was in a wheel chair woman would talk to me, wave, and smile. Now, I am on the walker nothing. Woman shy away, divert eyes, and don't smile. It is discouraging when I think of dating again. The asking out woman is not a problem it's my own fear of woman thinking I am broken. Being patient and persistence that I can do anything. Anything.

5:00 After Physical therapy we watched my nephew till mom got home after her rectification class which was 9PM. Off to bed.

March 14, 2008

Woke up at 6 am. Showered and ate breakfast by 8 am. Physical rehab at 9 am. Back at home I had a light lunch and slept for about four hours.

Worked most of the day from bed. Changes at home had to be made. Yes, I am scared for being on my own again. Having trauma is different in each case. There are still days where I cry at night, during the night, and wake up crying. I let the tears come. I feel so much release from crying.

We all have dreams, desires, goals, and we sometimes have trucks that get in our way of what we want to achieve. Someone may have a truck in the shape of trying to loose weight. I saw plenty of people who got knee replacements who were also very over weight. After awhile joints just can not handle it. Another truck may be in the form of a job you hate, a bad relationship, or an addiction.

I look at my accident as a blessing. It slowed me down, I learned scores of lessons, old lessons were reinforced, I became closer to my gods and who I prayed and meditated to.
Yes, some stuff came out that may not appear a blessing which was a direct result from trauma. I had to accept myself the way I was. This was key to be not so hard on my self or frustrated. Anger and other emotions came out as well. Coping with a trauma injury I find is never give up on your self. I got this far. Most of all I am loved scars visible and not visible.

Writing became a good way to release what was in my head. Words became a powerful tool to express my feelings. I started my journal soon as I was able to write. This came after all my tubes were pulled before leaving ICU. I continued with the blog on MySpace page at www.myspace.com/davidgerbstadt. (reader note: now blog on my face book page under my name)

For my sisters they began a journal while I was in ICU. I have yet to find that journal. Perhaps I am not to know the contents of what was written. They wrote from day one from their perspective.

This is my story and I will be as truth full as I can be. I may hurt someone cannot please everyone.

By compiling this book into fragments I have brought together a diverse grouping of ideas that that helped me not only survive but to continue on the best I can. Their will be moments I still cry for no other reason than to just cry.

I knew I had to go beyond this story in print and speak out to the public. That moment came the second time I was picked up and taken to physical therapy. I told the guy driving and he said he got goose bumps and was inspired by my speaking to him. He told me I should be a speaker "you would be real good at it!" I took it as the omen it was.

My thoughts are often of the accident. I did not think or wonder I just did what I did to stay alive.

March 15, 2008

DARN IT APPLESAUCE! Such a perfect phrase for today. Slept a tiny better. Strange dreams indeed. Took a shower to try and feel a little better. Breakfast of eggs and swiss cheese side of plain yogurt and fresh berries. Oh and orange juice! Plus, the pills though I really doubt they even work anymore.

Christine and her boy Alexander are off today to see the aquarium. I lie in bed in feet propped up mode typing away.

My mood is a notch or two on the depressed side. Basis of depression is fear of living life after experiencing death. I know I can be such a help to others and I have experienced some of this already. It feels good to know my horror can help someone else which lessens my trauma.

Ok. Best part of doing a journal entry book thang.... I can switch topics faster than instant pudding.

WHEN DID DUCKS START EATING BREAD! Darn it applesauce! Bread is not found in the wild. There are no stale white bread trees. There is a plant called bread fruit. That is what the ship the Bounty was carrying. You know that story or movie.

If you did not know already that story is true. Captain Bligh along with about a dozen loyal men were set adrift by the Bounty's mutinying crew. With only a few days of food and water, a sextant and a pocket watch. With out any charts or compass Captain Bligh navigated from what he learned from Captain Cook the 23 foot launch 3618 nautical miles to Timor. In only 47 days with only the loss of one crewmember who was killed on Tofua.

Captain Bligh kept a journal of the Launch voyage. Published with title: 'The Voyage of the Bounty Launch'.

Strange I can go from a duck to a mutiny in no time. What shall I write about next?

You got to love post trauma stress disorder (PTSD). We spoke to a psychologist in the hospital while still in ICU. Nightmares, sweating, sever trauma. I cried. The people at my bed side just stared, held my hand and said soothing things to me. All I saw was blood, terror, screaming. The nurse would come in my room smile and say you want… I would say yes give me the morphine. She would slip in 5ml. The pain would go someplace else. I would shut my eyes and trip my head off mostly good and some bad. Morphine was good for one thing knocking pain. It came with horrific trips as well. One I remember was a smiling mother holding her baby boy. She then took her fingers and poked the boys eyes out ramming the fingers all the way in. I would open my eyes and shut them this usually "reset" the trips. I would see the same smiling mother over and over. I would open my eyes and see smiling family members doing crossword puzzles or writing.

One night I saw my dad sleeping in a chair all night. He was not there. I saw all sorts of stuff like that. My mind was fooled to where I did not know what was real or not. My brother held my hand I cold feel the pressure smell the smell. I closed my eyes

Well, I did start telling everyone that this story is really a cover for something else…
Having a sex change. Won't they be surprised! Ha ha!

Actually, I would love to do reverse spam email. Every time I get a spam that sender gets 1,000 spam.

Sunday March 16, 2008

How about don't let perfection get in the way of progress.

Ok! So, I love someone! Have now for one and half years! I never told her. Never. How can I "love" someone with out even going out with the person. I just knew. When I saw them smiling at me I knew that I would be ok that day. Just felt so happy and warm.

All that in a small, nice, neat, smile. I hardly even spoke to her.

I was going to call her when I got to Florida. I was going to call her on Christmas Day. I never did. When I was nearing that truck I thought about calling her… Then I struck that truck! My thought of ever telling this girl how I felt quickly was slipping through my bloody hand. Her face slipped away as I died in the ambulance. Her face gone. I saw the light… I died.

I cried late at night in ICU. Her face came back in my mind… someplace in my wet tear face. I died 3 times that afternoon… My heart pumped and stopped. I remembered all that! I need someone to hold on to… After all my family left me at 8 pm every night while I was in ICU. I thought of her. My hands tied down. A vent tube down to my lungs, on a feeding tube, and several other tubes pulling blood out of my lungs and traps set up for preventing clots. Now, I was physically not able to call her now. Procrastination? You think so!

It would be an afternoon more than a month later... I got a card with her name signed that she missed me. I picked up the phone and called her... Another card came in the mail. She wrote saying she missed me a lot! Cheering me on with my recovery. I wheeled my chair out into the hallway with the card in my hand crying! The Nurses station being right across from my room had many Nurses come running! I handed one the card and could not speak I was crying so hard!

She later said, "I am sorry you had to go through this for us to start talking." She said, "we have to hang out together when you get home."

Many phone calls later I asked her out. She said, no. I asked if she wanted to still hang out. She said, yes of course!

Yes, my heart started to break a bit. How could it not. The gods have a plan. I just am not allowed to know the whole plan. I must trust and just let it unfold. It will all work out. I will not give up!

If I am not to be with this person so be it. I was with the gods most people do not ever see and are able to talk about it.

Monday, March 17, 2008

6:30 am: Been up for a while now. Got my five hours of sleep. Woke up with PAIN in leg and had to PEE! I did not use the bedside urinal and managed to get to the bathroom for relief and a glass of water to suck down some pain meds.

Today, is St. Patrick's Day. For some one who does not drink I just think it as an amateur day.

On to bigger smeller fish on the grill!

OK- LETS ROLL! As of now I do not have a job or insurance. Faxing paperwork over and over. Being lied to by every place I call or fax.

to make this easy- (yeah I am pissed off) place 1 needs medical records. So I call medical records to fax the records to place 1. easy huh? nope. call records back next day. Oh we did not fax that what's your name again? no we did not fax that. I call back several times. No we did not fax that. Finally after several days I am told it was faxed the very next day I requested it. Ha ha... oh it gets better that was just a warm up- Place 1 calls me saying I have no benefits.

I call HR ahhh well.... ok now I know I am sinking in poop. I learned before how to speak to them- ACT CALM NO F WORDS. And say- WHAT DO I NEED TO DO TO GET THIS DONE. Oh - fax this form to such and such. I did! 2 times already and HR called me last week saying this was taken care of in fact I asked if it was in fact done twice. they assured me it was done! HA HA HA.... AND they all call 10 minutes to 5 so I have to call back in the morning and my operation is this Thursday. HA HA HA HA.... AHHHH! I have to laugh and say where is that screw gun I will take out the screw in my knee and it won't cost $1,000 for 2-3 minute operation. OK so I may stripe the screw head. big deal I can just drill out the screw. BZZZZZZZZZZZZZZ!

GOING HOME

Thursday April 3, 2008

Flight: 699
Depart: Sarasota, FL 2:54 pm
Arrive: Atlanta, GA 4:29 pm
Gate: B12 Seat 20F (window)

Flight: 340
Depart: Atlanta, GA 5:17 pm
Arrive: Philadelphia 7:23 pm
Gate: D4 Seat 12A (window)

Made my flight 5 minutes before last call. I made it on board and to my seat. The two woman next to my seat got up and saw in my eyes I needed help. You need help? They said. "Yes I have an injury." Smiling can you put my bag up? One woman put my bag up into the overhead compartment. I thanked her and sat down. The woman looked at me wincing.

Are you ok? They asked. I had an accident... and told them the short version. The usual eyes wide open and dropped mouths. A few minutes later they moved behind me to the exit row leaving me to have 3 seats. I smiled and put my left leg up on the seats next to me.

The snack cart came by usually I pass on anything they offer. I just don't like making more trash than I need. This time I needed something to eat. Cranberry juice with ice and one half ounce of pretzels about the size of a dime. I counted 15 pretzels in all. Fishing out my touch IPod and selected some up beat music... Prince and Purple Rain. Perfect. Here I am 35,000 feet above the ground sipping juice with ice... As I sipped on the juice and popped a pretzel in my mouth I thought of the places on earth that did not have ice so readily available or good clean drinking water.

The flight was short. Perfect for my leg for it was having a parade on it's own. Nerve pain and spasms reminded me that it would be a long time to heal. The canker sore just on the inside top lip tried so hard to get top position for pain. When the juice hit the mouth sore it SCREAMED SAYING "HERE I AM! I BAD AND NASTY!" I just laughed and said that you will be gone in a short time... You have nothing on what is going on in my leg.

The plane touched down perfect landing! I clap as I always do when a plane touches down. Learned that landing in Puerto Rico where the locals all clap real loud and shout out "PUERTO RICO!" It gives a sense that home is more... it is love and pride where you live. I loved staying on the island for over a month and seeing how people lived. Not staying in some resort where you could be anywhere in the world with sunshine. Walking and being among the local residents is how I like to travel. I see how they live in brightly colored houses and the school children wear uniforms... oh and the piraguas! A snow cone.

Called this because they are made in pyramid shapes and "agua" means water in Spanish; hence the name "pir-agua". We would buy this flavorful cool treat from street vendors. Two days before I left we went to a street fair and had a grape snow cone. Taste so good in 85 degree weather. We have to thank the inventor Ernest Hansen who patented the first known "Ice block shaver" in New Orleans, Louisiana in 1934.

Walking through the jet way a sharp cold breeze penetrated into my leg. This air caused a parade in my leg that went in front of the judge's stand giving it all it had!

Coming out of the gate into the terminal I saw I had only to go a couple gates to mine. Yes!

The Atlanta flight was just a repeat show only difference was the 12 planes lined up nose to tail. Yes, it was 5 o'clock rush hour for take off. Once leveled off again at 35,000 feet.

The Captain of the plane said over the pa system "we are now 450 miles from Philadelphia". I started feeling the love that got me through the accident. The solid lump in my throat came… tears forth coming. Then the love wrapped around my body. That same moment the snack cart appeared!

I choose the same order of juice and pretzels. The bag of pretzels had printed on the front "How to eat gourmet pretzels" I thought they sure were gourmet these suckers cost me $210. Let's see 2 bags of pretzels 15 in each bag plus 2 juices. Hmm… if I had just the pretzels. I would cost me $7 per pretzel.

That is a damn good mark up!

The directions to eat pretzel were on the back… so with some time to kill I flipped over the bag.

Eating instructions:

1. Think about your wonderful low fares at AirTran.com as you open packet.
2. Place pretzel in mouth. With each crunch, be reminded of our low fares.
3. As you swallow, remember again just how low the fares are.
4. Repeat till pretzels packet is empty.
5. Keep empty packet to remind yourself to book at AirTran.com for our low fares. And no booking fees.

Take the trash with me? So the airline can save on trash bags and disposing of trash what a great idea someone thought of to save money.

My feelings coming home…

Lack of emotions
Sad
Choked up
Sentimental
Thankful

Scared
Sighing
Thinking
Burping at 35,000 feet
Wonder what it is like to burp in space

My life simply does not feel "real". I feel that I was an alien beamed down to earth before the accident. Now, I know I am not from this world... truly. I have been grown into a new life. Love and dreams is just how it is supposed to be... I hear and see this accident as a blessing. If I can heal and remain sober I can be a lighthouse for many more.

People say they admire me, look up to me, tell me I am a hero... Someone who just did what I did.

The captain comes back on the pa system, "in 14 minutes we will be on the ground". This is the captains plan.

I regard my self as just being. I do see great things ahead of me... The plan is to speak for groups and organizations. Going to tell the story of survival, hope, love, never give up... even when you have no breath no heart beat... nothing.

Coping and living one day at a time with my new found life new found journey. There is nothing I can not do.

You can do what ever your dream is... Do not let any person or situation tell you can not do it. They may say you will fail. If you do fail so what? Keep on trying! Never give up!

I hope to see you on the trail... Keep on keeping on!

Write issues out on paper to god---
What am I wondering about--- its' real on paper and review –

People –

How to draw a spirit house--- (bird houses) giving it out to the gods and universe

HOME

One phone call to the airline, and I had a return ticket paid using the credit from my old ticket. With $4.80 cents left over.

John: I regard you as an artist, pure and simple, doing your art. Who cares where you go for money as a job. Your art is what defines you and makes you real. People love your art and what you are doing! If your art is writing right now... then it is writing. You are needed.

Needed? As beat up inside as I feel physically and emotionally, I am needed? Yes, why else would the kids of the local elementary school send over 200 art post cards to you, why would you get cards and letters, balloons, candy, and more gifts, visits...

It was not the material or actual visits that made me cry. It was the fact that the thoughts and prayers were sent...

As for physically walking in my house again after 3 months... it all seemed foreign. The idea I had to paint the walls and change things was even more difficult to me. I was sick to see what my roommate had done as "changes." I was sick to see even more of a mess after being in an orderly and sterile environment at the hospital. I grew depressed.

WHY DOES THE WORLD NEED THIS BOOK?

This question was raised by my publisher, my agent, and by others in the world of words…. I simply set forth to write what had to come out. Blood, blood, blood, and more blood. According to Canadian Blood Services, a unit of blood is approximately 450 milliliters. The amount of blood in one person is equivalent to five liters, or ten and a half pints. On average, 4.6 units of blood are required per receiving patient. I had forty units of fluid pumped through me between the scene of the accident and the moment I came out of surgery. I required another twenty-one units over the couple of days that followed. Sixty-one units in all. That is equal to nearly forty-three gallons of blood.

PART 2

To cope and to continue to live, I kept writing and made art....
Here is what I used:

>sketch book
>note book
>rice box sketch book

> Once an idea, image, or word is transferred to a surface,
> it's there to be seen and remembered!

How many times during your days at work, driving in the car, or doing anything else in your life do you think and have a feeling or an IDEA! You owe it to yourself to jot these thoughts down so later you can refer to them and do with them as you please....

So now what? Get yourself a notebook that that you can carry around with you—something that fits your world. I have a friend who cuts up his rice boxes and uses the cardboard for the backs of his sketchbooks. Just decide on the size you want and cut plain paper into smaller pages. Then take two pieces of cardboard from a food box and cut them to be a little larger than your pages. At the top of one of the pieces of cardboard, score a line about half an inch down from the top. Use a binder clip to clip the pages together. This way, you can easily add or take away pages.

Other easy solutions are marbled composition books or any other type of notebook. On my walks, I have even found books in trash cans lying right on top of the garbage.... I have used these books and drawn right over the printed text.

Found books such as these are discovered in laundromats, thrift shops, garage sales, or even on your own bookshelf. To go over printed text is not a fresh concept.... Artists have used newspaper, phonebooks, novels, and a variety of other materials to create something new.

Once you have your OWN book to use however you want—a story, song, painting, play, movie script, or whatever—the next thing to do is to carry it with you. Take it everywhere—on the train or bus, in your car, waiting for the doctor....

The idea is to release some of the ideas you have onto paper so you can remember them and use them later.... The step after that would be actually making your idea a reality by bringing it off of the pages and into the world for more people to enjoy.

THE ACT OF DRAWING!

Drawing is moving a pen, pencil, crayon—or really anything that can make a mark—on paper.

In college, it took one teacher to tell me I was swimming in the deep end—in other words, he said that I was good at art! It took just one person to make me aware I was worthy of something. Up to that point, I had no idea I was 'good' at anything....

I took his advice and continued farther out into deeper water. Then I had to take DRAWING CLASS! This was a groan and moan, and many can relate to that. Why? The idea of making it 'LOOK' like the posed model, still life, or landscape is a problem. Many people complain,"I can't even draw a stick figure!"

I didn't die as a result of figure drawing, though, and I walked out of the art building with the idea that I didn't have to draw the way somebody else draws—I will draw the way I draw! It's my way, and my teachers saw that I was doing my own thing and not just running through the motions of trying to PLEASE them.

This idea took hold most strongly in my lithograph print-making class, which I saved for the end of my tour of duty at college. The instructor was a master printer, and his drawings were mind-blowing in the faculty shows each year. I gained the strength and knowledge at this point to walk into his class and hold nothing back!

There were several cliques from which I could have found people to talk to.

There was a girl who literally stood in the corner doing something I could never quite figure out. All I know is that she said she'd had this teacher before and had been failed the first time through his class. She kept muttering, "I just don't know what he wants...."

I steered well clear of her—she would only bring me down.

Then there were the flashy academic artists who were from downtown Lancaster and really had nothing interesting to talk about....

So I just made my own clique and drew!

Now, the process was quite involved for this class. If you didn't come in to work at least two nights a week after class time, you were automatically assigned a C grade.

Preparing the stone for the manual presses took the most time—several weeks. I was required to make six different stones and a set numbered run for each print. Do the math, I had a ton of work on my hands....

My first print was a self portrait—a dark face with white eyes peering out. An early and dark image. The second one was a self-awareness put down with text.... And I just did what I damn well cared to do!

It wasn't until I was into my third stone—many weeks into the 15-week course—that my teacher spoke directly to me! He said, "Well, it was good you told everyone to fuck off in your last print! It behooves you to know that I am going to pour a LARGE MARTINI tonight!"

I was in shock that the man spoke beyond technique to me and his general address to the class... I was in a daze and left the class needing to take a moment for myself in the hallway. Was I on to something? What the hell did he mean—told everyone to fuck off! Hmmm....

So I returned to my stone and completed it. I literally scribbled all over the entire fourteen by sixteen inch stone. In these scribbles, I pulled out figures that represented my lithography class. I was depicted as a conductor with a baton, and on the music stand perched a tiny bird. Some of my fellow students were seated at tables, smoking and drinking in a jazz club. Others played instruments. And there was my teacher, sitting upon a big mushroom with a HUGE martini glass.

The teacher said to me while I was printing it up, "This would look good on black paper with white ink."

I told him I had not ordered black paper in the bulk order with the class.

He then lead me into his office, where he peeled out a sheet some fifty inches long of black arches paper that was worth a few dollars. "Here, use this," he said, and he didn't take any money for it.

I ran two prints with white ink. It was not till the end of the term that I was walking through the open gallery in the building, when I passed my same print in the student show! I froze, double backed, and stared at my print hanging right there on the wall! My teacher never asked or even told me about it—it was just there!

At that moment, I knew I had gotten an A in his class. In fact, I did get an A and proved to myself that DRAWING is what you WANT IT TO BE! JUST DRAW AND MOVE THE PEN ON THE PAPER! That is all there is to drawing. And if you want to get better, just keep drawing! You can't do it wrong, and you can always do it better.

162 | One Breath At A Time

Litho Print: Self Portrait

THE BUDDY SYSTEM – MENTOR/GOOD FRIEND

If you have just one GOOD friend, then you are very lucky....

Whether something okay, good, great, or something that is stinky-malinky happens in your life, the experience is always better when you have someone to share it with. I am lucky that I have two good friends—one male, who is an artist, and one female, who is also creative. We talk on the phone nearly every day, even though the conversations may literally last only a few seconds....

"Just checking in with my good friend David. You okay?"

I generally say "yes" or provide short details of the latest, and the caller then usually comes back with his or her own short details.

Our calls are often quick and to the point—no fluff. We both know that what we have to say is helping the other, and we honor and cherish our friendships.

There are countless times when human waste has hit the fan and we need to call someone to help defuse the issue. Usually, it's the simple act of talking our problems out that helps us realize our "issue" or "problem" is merely ant poop and that we are OKAY!

One of my friends does not use email and, out of personal choice, has no computer, so the phone is an instant and much better way to get a hold of him.

By talking about life's 'details' and our art, we have learned that nothing is too bad. With a friendship like that, life is much less stressful, and bumps do not turn into mountains.... They are just bumps.

ACTION

The more you talk and think about doing something, then the farther you get from actually doing it!

> Press on nothing in the world can take the place of persistence. Talent will not; nothing is more common than unsuccessful men with talent. Genius will not; unrewarded genius is almost a proverb. Education will not; the world is full of educated derelicts. Persistence and determination alone are omnipotent.
>
> — Coolidge

How often have people wanted to do something, but the worry of not having enough talent or education has stopped them from even trying to do it?

I had the opportunity to work with someone who kept telling me to sell more paintings. He told and retold the story of an author who used to work on a manual typewriter in a trailer with several kids running around. He pressed shirts at a drycleaning shop, and his wife worked twelve-hour days at a doughnut shop. Their phone was cut off, and he would have to take his calls at a payphone.

One day, this writer got a call from his agent, who said, "I sold one of your stories for $400,000."

The connection was not good, though, and the writer answered, "Four hundred dollars? Great! I could use the money!"

The agent repeated himself, "NO, I SAID $400,000!"

That writer was Steven King.

My coworker would routinely hold up a sheet of paper and pen and say, "All writers need is this to write anything they want! Anything!"

I added the word PATIENCE to my mantra, and I keep it in mind as I strive to keep on keeping on.

Sometimes, though, a break is needed to recharge.

Sometimes, many months went by without a painting sold—or even without making a single brush stroke…. But the thought of persistence remained in the back of my mind! Over time, I have learned that these breaks are a normal part of the creative process—to sit at a café or some other place with an Italian Soda and watch the world go by was part of the process.

Returning from a break to creating art again, I would have a new perspective on subjects and ideas. Time and time again, my persistence has paid for itself in more ways that can be expressed in words or medium—it stands alone and should be understood as such.

My friend calls it "winding the magnet." Everything you do winds another coil of wire around a steel rod to create a wire magnet. Some people give up after only a few wraps—perhaps they don't believe anything will ever happen. But the fact is that something is happening—sometimes gradually and sometimes quickly. The wires gain mass and begin to act as powerful magnet….

Things begin to happen! The phone rings, mail is received, and people come into your life that are drawn in by your magnetic pull. This has happened countless times for the artists who I honour and respect in their practice of persistence. It has also happened to me.

Love what you do and do what you love….

Now close your eyes and think of one thing that you like to do or WISH you could do. Maybe you would like to…TAP DANCE! Well, then, just do it! My mother was sixty-eight years of age when she started taking tap dancing classes. Why? Because, when she was a little girl, she had wanted to take tap, but her family could not afford it. In fact, she had to start working at an age so young she had to lie about it. Time passed, and she married, raised four children, and moved several times. Only later in life did she decide to take up lessons and make her childhood dream a reality by dancing on stage at a recital with other women her age. Such tremendous joy she expressed that day.

SWEEP AND STARE AT THE WALL

When an artist feels not able to hold a pen, brush, or any other drawing instrument, he might begin to doubt himself. Thoughts pour into his world of wide ideas that are simply not true. Whispers of nothing seep into creating nothing....

And this is OKAY!

Step back, grab a broom, sweep the floor, park your butt, and stare at the wall in the studio. Just sit in the studio in silence or with some music playing. The key concept is to SIT and do nothing—which, actually, is something. Your mind might race with thoughts of countless other tasks you could be doing instead of just sitting.

If you have not done this, though, it is a way to clear the mind and focus on nothing. My friend does this, and she has told me it's all part of the process to step back and just spend time in the place you create. The important part, she says, is to be in your studio so when an idea comes you are ready to ACT!

I do this as well. I wake up, and before I leave for my day job I go to just sit among the materials. Leaving the space does something to the mind and body that I cannot express. I just feel a lot better after sitting than before.

BUMPS IN THE ROAD

We all have experienced bumps in the road of life. Family members are diagnosed with cancer, die, or suffer from other tragic circumstances. Sometimes, the bumps are self-inflicted and our own doing. We sometimes lie or bring about our own self-destruction. People make mistakes. We are not perfect. There are things we can control and that we perhaps could change. But we have to be willing to change. Only then can progress be made.

People in marriage and relationships sometimes hurt or make each other MAD! A married friend of mine told me this after I had admitted I'd screwed up! She said, "What you did is really a bump in the road!" She said, "It's like going to a tropical island for vacation, and it does not rain. You think it's that perfect all the time! And you want to move there without realizing that it does rain in paradise."

I told her, "I see your point."

She added, "Hurricanes come through and wipe out everything, and the people there rebuild. It may take time to rebuild, but, with action, it is rebuilt. There are many bumps in marriage. Years later, these bumps are forgotten about or even laughed at. There are also smooth roads in relationships, and it is all part of the journey."

SITTING AND WATCHING THE WORLD GO BY

Once in a while, put down the pen, brush, or whatever you are using and go to a café. Order a beverage, and watch the world go by…

Taking a break, observing, and recharging your batteries is all a part of the creative process. Turn the phone off. Don't worry about the pending ISSUES you may have. One or two hours don't matter in most cases. It's not wasting time—it is balancing work with pleasure.

Breathe and take notice of sounds, sights, and anything else that appeals to your senses. Smile. Enjoy the moment for simply being the moment.

Sounds odd to just be sitting and doing nothing? Why?

"I MUST BE DOING SOMETHING!" you say? "PRESS ON!"

Sure, you could. But then what? What have you learned and taken in about yourself and your surroundings? Try to SIT and just exist for the time it takes to drink your beverage. Don't drink while walking or driving your car. Just sit and watch the world go by….

CINCH BY THE INCH

When faced with monumental tasks, I break the task at hand into a list of smaller tasks that are easy.

Once one small task is done, I draw a line through it. That simple act of crossing provides a tremendous sense of accomplishment. You might even do this when buying food. You write a list and cross out or check the item off.

My father spent over five years building a thirty-nine-foot sailboat in his drive way. He started with a fiberglass hull and deck. He listed many tasks, and each one was crossed out upon completion.

A trial by the mile may be hard by the yard, but it's a cinch by the inch.

LAUGH AND BE SILLY

A hospice nurse came into work one day. She was picking up meds for a patient and said to me, "If I can make them laugh in their final few days, it's one of the best things I can do to make the transition of dying easier.

"Laugh and be silly!" She kept saying that as she left. She was so light-hearted and happy, even though she had to see people die on a regular basis.

After she left, I wrote down what she said to me.

She was right! Laughter is the best medicine we have! Laughing and being silly is a good way to reduce stress and quiet the thoughts that may worry us. Most problems are purely ant poop, and in a week or two we forget why we were upset or worried in the first place.

A fellow artist friend and I did a collaborative painting. At the top of it, she wrote, "Happiness is a decision."

Abe Lincoln once said, "Most people are about as happy as they make up their minds to be."

Sure, we cannot be HAPPY all the time! We feel grief, sorrow, pain, loss, anger, jealousy, and so on…. The important thing is to not stay in that emotion so long so it controls you and rents free space in your head!

Forgiving yourself and others is a good way to get over something quickly. I am not perfect by any means. I have hurt people, and people have hurt me. Through pain, trust is lost. But everyone has feelings, and forgiveness is a good way for people to move through the mistrust.

Forgiving yourself for screwing up may be hard. But just keep saying to yourself, "I forgive myself!" After a while, you will be at ease and begin to LAUGH again and, yes, be silly!

There is an old proverb that says life is way too short to take yourself so seriously! Don't get caught up thinking so hard. Write your thoughts down and destroy what you wrote. Draw. Take a long walk on your own... The right action will lead you to right thinking and bring a sense of calm over you.

BEAMED DOWN

Since I was young and able to see and understand my surroundings, I've felt different, alone, and outcast. It took many years before I was able to accept that I was different—that feeling that I was beamed down from another planet and that everything is odd and people are all strangers. I kept this idea all to myself for a long time.

Then I met someone when I was about twenty-seven years old. He told me he felt as though he had been beamed down on to earth. Reciting a quote from the novel *Out of Africa*, "He made friends among strangers, always longing in his heart for the distant cry of his home."

Being different is a feeling that the two of us share, and, over the years, we have found others who have also been beamed down to earth. It does not make us any better or worse than others—it just is what it is. I still feel this way. As a jazz singer/songwriter I know says, "I am different, and I don't give a damn."

Not just artists, musicians, writers, and thinkers feel this way, I have found. I know a doctor who woke from a nightmare so vivid and powerful that he is using it to write a book. The dream was just so shocking that something had to be done with it.

We are perhaps all strangers at one point or another in our lives. We are never really alone.

DO WHAT YOU LOVE
LOVE WHAT YOU DO

I am astonished by my ability to remember exact places and things said to me by other people. One night at yet another drinking party, a classmate came over to me. He said, "You're the only one who I know here at school who is doing what you love! The other people here are going straight after money! You're doing it!"

I remember what he said because he was one hundred percent right! Only he did not know I HAD to make art! I was not thinking, "Hmm, perhaps I should paint today...." Rather, I thought, "I MUST PAINT TODAY!" If I didn't paint, I truly felt dead. So I painted! I love what I do and do what I love—I make art! And I have experimented with many forms and mediums.

I explored, grew, and developed as an artist. In doing so, I also expanded my general knowledge and met many people. I explored different ways of painting, as well and talked with people who paint with mud and earth and people who paint with spray cans. I found others with the same passion and drive I had, only they were using different materials. The outcome was the same, though! We made art!

SNACK TIME

When we were young and in school, we would have snack time and receive some juice or milk and cookies or pretzels. Our growing minds needed something to run on in the afternoon. When we got home, we might have needed another snack before dinner—we were so hungry!

I remember getting home from grade school at three or four in the afternoon. I was so hungry by then that I could eat a snack before dinner and have no problem finishing dinner. Now, I have what I call three o'clock snack time. My snack consists of something small—perhaps a piece of fruit or something comforting that can fuel my creative mind until dinner.

"It's three o'clock snack time!" By saying it out loud, I become connected to my inner child and am reminded that I am fragile and need to take care of myself.

MUFFIN WITH FRIEND

How we begin our day is vital to how the rest of the day will progress. I found that by starting the day with my friend in a muffin shop before work did both of our hearts a world of good. We simply take a half hour to talk about life and perhaps about the ups and downs we face, art, quotes and ideas from books, and our experiences that have meaning. This helps simplify our lives and decreases our stress. Just being in the moment with someone before you begin your day can set the tone for the entire day.

Being mindful and aware of the present moment is all we have. The kind of morning meetings I have with my friend gives me the opportunity to release what is on my mind to another person who I trust and like. The food we eat together fuels our bodies and comforts our souls. Together, we record key moments in words or drawings that capture the present, allowing us to go back when we choose.

After we finish our muffins and drinks, our meeting is over, and we must part our separate ways. Taking that time to stop and just be in the moment has made my life more manageable, less stressful, and leaves me with a warming energy to see the world in different ways.

SEEING OUT THE WINDOW

> Looking: Light passes through the lens of the eye, and the vitreous humor, hits the retina, which stimulates rods (B/W) & cones (color) to send images are sent along the optic nerve.
>
> Seeing: The brain actually processes the information, based upon prior knowledge, and assigns meaning to the images received.

Everyday, we look at thousands of images. These images are so ingrained that they may simply disappear. But actually seeing images that make up our everyday lives brings what may have been overlooked out into the light. Change is a constant, never-ending process. My friend says, "The shit keeps flowing." Through our daily phone conversations, he points out that I keep moving forward without giving up!

There was a time when the idea of giving up sounded attractive. My days consisted of lying on the couch, filled with dread and worry of even the simplest of errand to go buy postage stamps.

What brought me out of such a severely depressed state of mind without medication? First, I visualized myself leaving the couch and going to a particular location step by step—a journey in my mind to where I wanted to go. Then I began to look out the window and slowly take notice of the life out there. Birds and squirrels darting around became relaxing to look at and gave me a sense of calm. Slowly, I let the light that I saw trickle into my body and warm me. The light brought to the surface a life I knew was there all along....

The transformation was slow, and people around me smiled as they watched me step into the light. They commented on the change I made from a dark and severely depressed person into someone who was full of life and outgoing.

They said it was good to know the real me.

By seeing out the windows of our lives, looking out into the world, we can see the world for what it is. Good or bad, it is all part of our changing lives. Take note of what you are seeing and know that you are part of it.

KILL THEM WITH KINDNESS

Along my journey, I chose jobs that gave me the freedom to think while also working as an artist. When I worked in a pharmacy, a woman, who also worked with the public and understood how hard it sometimes is to serve, told me, "I KILL THEM WITH KINDNESS! No matter if they drop the F-BOMB at you for no reason or treat you like crap! I just smile and kill them with kindness."

I took her words to heart. After a long day of people literally throwing their credit cards at me or greeting me with hostility, I just smiled and tried to kill them with kindness. Upon encountering a customer who was repeatedly rude and nasty, I just took a deep breath and remained calm.

LIFE WITH OUT MUSIC IS A MISTAKE

After over forty years of programming computers, my father retired. He started his career by plotting satellites for the government in the late 1950s and early 60s. He ended his career working with the early stages of voice recognition communications.

He worked hard to support four kids and a wife, and music was always played in our house—GOOD music, as he would say, and he would quote The Duke: "If it sounds good, it is good!"

As a retirement present to himself, he bought a piano, and, unless he is away from home, he now plays for several hours every day. Sure, he admits he is not 'good,' but this does not stop him, and he continues to play! It's in the playing that he feels absolute joy and passion, and he strives to play better each time he sits down.

He tells me that life without music is a mistake and that music, art, and literature are vital parts of life that resonate in the very core of our souls as human beings.

THIS IS NOT A BRAIN TUMOR

If a problem can be solved, there is no use worrying about it. If the problem cannot be solved, there is also no use worrying.

Time and money fix a lot of our 'problems.' I like to call them situations. This too shall pass—"like bad gas," I think when I am faced with a situation. If it is not a brain tumor, then it's not worth the space it takes in your head to worry. Just do the next right thing, and, when the day is over, you can breathe with the knowledge it was a good day because you did what you could.

I have solved many 'problems' by doing nothing at first. I step back, do something else, and then return to the original problem.

Sometimes, taking care of the problem a little at a time is faster than trying to take care of it all at once. Little tasks comprise a big task.

LOSING SIGHT

Don't worry about the road ahead—just get as far as you can today, and you'll be able to get farther in the morning.

When you get discouraged by the road ahead, turn around and look how far you have come. You don't always have to go forward. You can keep going, turn back around, or change direction. Sometimes, you might lose sight of your path and need to be pointed in the right direction. If no one helps you, then turn around and retrace your steps....

A friend's daughter complained that she was not DOING anything or getting ANYTHING done! He suggested writing down every task she completes on a notecard and then putting those notecards in a box. Very quickly, the box filled up with cards that reassured her that she was, indeed, DOING something.

When we forget how good we are, being reminded in a small way is helpful to our egos. Often, we get too caught up in negative thinking when we are unsure. This negative thinking can completely eclipse positive thinking. We, as humans, are our own worst critics.

Then a friend, family member, or even a strager makes an encouraging comment, and these comments tend to be remembered for a long time.

As an artist, I have received hundreds of negative comments. Some of these comments can be found in guest books from my shows. Most of the time, they are not written with any truth or concrete backing, and rarely are they signed. In fact, one comment was so far off that I wondered if the person actually saw the painting they wrote about. They just wanted to say something horrible! They even went as far as to claim I was not a citizen and that my moral issues were questionable.

That particular painting was made very late one night while on the phone with another artist. The conversation went like this, "I don't care! I am going to try it this way!" And after a few hours on the phone and nearly seeing the sun rise, the result was a major breakthrough with my art.

Most people, upon seeing that painting, loved it and told me so. Everyone wanted to buy it. Now, I only laugh at the one bad comment that was ever made about it. Everyone has their own spin on what they see. That critic never spoke to me in person about my work, so he or she never knew that what they said was not even in my mind at the time.

RULES FOR PLAY

In my studio is a large sheet of paper. Written on it in colored pencil and crayon is a list with the heading, "RULES FOR PLAY!" It is a gentle reminder to not take my life so seriously and to play.

It is through play that I learn about myself, my surroundings, and other people. Often, people think I am far younger than I really am—not by maturity but by appearance.

1. Smile and laugh
2. Smile and grab someone's hand
3. Eat: Grilled cheese sandwiches
    Macaroni and cheese
    Hot pretzels
    Ice cream
    Pizza
    Milkshakes
    Brownies
4. Eat Chinese food late at night and save the fortune in the cookie to put on the refrigerator
5. Drink tea afterwards
6. Ride your rainbow
7. Play records
8. Do what you liked doing when you were a kid
9. Wear a funny hat
10. Just play

NEVER SAY CAN'T

In college, I pledged for a national fraternity. During pledging, I was drilled on certain quotes or ideas. One that stuck with me was "never say can't!"

The brothers did not want to hear us ever using that word! They wanted to see us complete our tasks! Every night, we had study hour, during which we all ganged together, read, and studied our courses. There were fifteen of us working together as a unit for six weeks.

One morning, I realized I had lost my wallet the night before. Within a few minutes, there were over six guys searching through the area where I had been. Very quickly, someone found my wallet—and it was a nylon-camouflaged wallet, too! When one of us had a problem, the others helped.

Today, if I am faced with a situation, I remember never to say can't. There is no excuse for not asking for help. Asking for help does not make someone weaker or inferior—they just do not know how to do something on their own.

KEEP ON FUNKING ON

There is no way of doing art—or anything creative, for that matter—wrong. How can we even question such a process? If we are wrong, then our god or higher power is wrong.

Keep funking on is an idea that has been used by many creative souls throughout time. Beethoven became filled with suicidal thoughts after a critic wrote poorly about his music. He came out of it, though, and said, "I shall create for god and god alone."

I know many artists who do not display their art. They are not shy about or unsure of the worthiness of their art. Rather, they are comfortable with themselves, create for the sake of creating, and find pure joy in simply that. By getting up and just doing something or anything in the studio with pen, camera, brush, or instruments, they "funk along."

Art prevails throughout and during hardships as it also does through good times. As an artist, I may be not always be physically working on my own art. Mentally, though, I am coming up with ways and ideas.

Having an active mind that is able to flow and think freely allows me to live as an artist, even if I am not physically making something.

People often comment on my level of energy as a person and artist. They are drawn to me, and I am introduced to others this way. The way others see me as an artist is not something I try to think about much.

CHRISTINE

After my sister Christine graduated from Penn State University in less than four years, she left home with only six hundred dollars and her Honda hatchback. She drove from Pennsylvania to Berkley University in California to get her Master's.

She had some lean times, and it was a gutsy thing to just go without much money. But she worked hard!

When she graduated from Berkley University, she went back to the East Coast for medical school. I remember she had to move home and would often fall asleep on a bed that was covered in heavy medical books. Her debt grew to over $300,000, and her only way to pay it off was to become a doctor!

Today, Christine is a doctor and a spokesperson for both the American Dietetic Association and the American Medical Association. She has articles published in Self Magazine and has been featured in USA Today newspaper.

She never gave up!

LOVED ONES DYING

December 14, 2006
1:20 PM

As I left the house I kissed my mom on the forehead… I went for onions to make enchiladas.

When I pulled into the drive way I just knew mom had her last breath.

As an artist to see my mother slowly die from cancer… Tears of many… Tears of joy… Everyone dies. I knew her time was luck.

How did I manage? How did I cope? How did I… Writing, making art, talking to friends, doing the next thing…

I just put one foot in front of the other.

Breathing.

We all die. We know how to die when the time comes.

We are not alone in this.

FEEL WHAT YOU FEEL

You probably have heard the saying, "Feelings are not facts." If they were, they would have been on the tests we took in school. Instead, we have to learn about feelings on our own.

First, experience the feeling! If you feel like you are going to cry and you don't know why, then just cry. If you are mad, be mad! That goes for whatever emotion you're feeling—let it out! Let it out and then let it go. Return to yourself. Do not stay trapped in that feeling.

We have felt anger, frustration, fear, resentment, greed, lust, heartbreak, and many more emotions.

If these feelings grip or remain inside of you, they own you. If they prevent you from sleeping or making the right decisions, they control your life.

How do we manage?

We manage by accepting whatever is causing these feelings and then just letting go. This may not be easy! Just keep trying.

Remember my fear of sleep because I dreaded the reoccurring nightmares? Those nightmares owned my sleep! To take back it back, though, I had to tell the nightmares to GO AWAY because I was in charge! And it worked!

This example may not work for you. My friend, who also has PTSD, has tried other methods, such as white noise and reading. Finally, he found that listening to classical music at a very low volume worked. Another friend discovered that by having a peanut butter and jelly sandwich with glass of milk an hour before bed puts him to sleep.

I am not perfect. We all learn from our feelings, sometimes quickly and sometimes after a while. Remember, though, progress not perfection.

FIND SOMEONE YOU TRUST AND TELL YOUR FEELINGS TO THEM

This may save your life one day, or it may save someone else's life. My friend told me once that a simple phone call just to say hello was enough for the other person to reconsider suicide that day. My friend did not know the other person wanted to commit suicide. Only much later, after the person got help, did he confront my friend to tell him that he was about to kill himself when he called.

Find someone you trust and get along with. Confide in him or her. Communicate your feelings. That way, when you really need to reach out, that call will be easier and might just save your life or someone else's.

JOURNAL OR WRITE SOMETHING
(This book helped bring closure for me.)

Take a notebook, open a Word document, or start a blog. Try to make an effort to write something or anything down—it could be just one word or sentence. It does not matter what you write. Write down your thoughts, feelings, and great ideas. There is no RIGHT WAY to write. Like drawing, you can just write whatever comes to mind. Do not stress over what to write. Just start writing. Do it daily, weekly, monthly, or whenever you have the chance. This is your own thing. Do it your way. Carry a small notebook and jot what stands out during the day.

You may ask, "Why bother? I hate to write."

What is holding you back? You do not have to show anyone what you have written. It is yours. You can even delete it or burn it. Putting a word down is a way of clearing the mind of clutter and helping you realize how free you really are.

Here are some questions to help you start writing:

1. If you are a parent, what has been really difficult as a parent today?
2. If you have no children, what one thing really made the day difficult for you?
3. What did you learn from this experience?
4. How have you helped your child and family today?
5. How did you feel today?
6. The best thing about your child is....
7. The worst thing about your child is....
8. The best part of the day is....
9. The worst part of the day is....
10. The best part of your spouse is....
11. The worst part of your spouse is....
12. The nicest thing said to you lately was....
13. Something that was very funny today was....
14. Something that was very sad today was....

GIVE YOURSELF A BREAK

We are not perfect. We may think we can handle work, family, or anything else that adds to our day. This builds up and wears down the body. In time, we might snap at the kids, feel tired during the day, and sense pressure from others.

Step back and take a break. No time? Only five minutes of quiet might make a difference in your day.

In my case, I was stuck in the ICU of the hospital. I had tubes pulling blood out of both my lungs, traps collecting more blood so I wouldn't clot. All this blood was drained out and collected into plastic bags that I could see. My hands were tied to the bedrails to prevent me from yanking out the tubes and wires. There was a tube in my throat that delivered oxygen. There was a tube that ran up my nose, down my throat, and into my stomach to feed me. Another tube delivered blood into my body. Overall, I was a mess!

Do you think I gave myself a break? No way! My family had been given a board with letters on it. They would untie my wrists and let me tap the letters to form words. After a sentence or two, they noticed how hard I was being on myself. They would then tie my hands again, and the nurse would come back in and give me more morphine to put me out.

Later, when I moved up to a wheelchair, I also had to be reminded to lighten up and give myself a break…. I wanted to do everything and got frustrated that I could not do it. I just had to accept what happened and where I was.

It was easy to wake up in the ICU. Coping with the accident, though, is still a work in progress. By talking to friends, writing about it, and being honest with myself, I continue to survive the trauma.

PLAY

Go ahead, go play! Get yourself a toy fire truck, some building blocks, or a water rocket! It is time to raid your kids' toy box and take some! You did pay for them, after all. If you don't like raids, well, then ask to borrow some toys. If you get a big NO, then try to trade for them. Tell them anything! Tell them they will get television time, candy—anything! Your mission is to get that toy!

Now, as a last resort, just cruise on down to the toy store and buy yourself something! Find something that you think is fun, cool, and makes you happy! Explore and pick up those HUGE PLASTIC DINOSUARS! Give them noises! Have them eat the dolls. Or play with the dolls! Put on a puppet or two and give them voices. Race the trucks. Go have a tea party! Believe me, laughing and playing is allowed in a toy store. I have done this and have yet to be kicked out. I even have been dressed as a clown, and they did not kick me out!

Choose your toy, take it to the counter, and pay for it. By all means, decline the bag. Now go out and play!

When you are done, give your toy away to a child or an adult. Or just put it on your shelf and play with it again later.

LAUGH

Laughter was heard on a regular basis on the rehab floor of the hospital. Finding humor in the everyday mundane of pain while we dealt with our new lives was a way of coping through the trauma.

Rent a funny movie, learn some jokes—there can be humor in any everyday situation.

Laughing releases the energy that is balled up inside the body.

CONSCIOUS STATE OF MIND

As someone who has suffered trauma and survived something that most people do not live through, my understanding and consciousness has gone to a dark place that many never experience. To continue on with my life, I must release that state of mind. To truly heal, I must not try to control the accident. I only had to do that one time—and that was at the moment of most critical need. I do not have to continue to relive the trauma. This only creates instability and anxiety that results in sleeplessness or a decrease in function as a human being.

By letting go and being part a fellowship already is of great importance to me. A level of trust has been established among a core group of people who have gone through extreme trauma.

Now what if someone is not in a fellowship or organization—what then? We all need human contact and understanding from people who have gone through similar situations. All you need is one person to trust and confide in. More people will come into your life—you just have to be open to them.

The more you speak of feelings and emotions to people who have 'been there,' the better you will feel. It is important to set boundaries and limits on people who are not in the core group you trust or can confide in. Pity is not useful to us, and submissiveness is a sickness in one who has been traumatized.

YOUR STORY

We as humans, we all have our own stories, and we own our stories. They are ours. Living in the present moment is the way to create a positive, more nurturing life. If we continue to live in our past or future, we lose sight of the actual moment as it occurs.

Being present in the here and now may be challenging at first. Slowing entering into a new way of thinking will create more stability and harmony in your life. It is not just a matter of being calm. I believe it goes beyond that into a relaxed state of mind.

We will have tough days and good days. The day is ours as we walk or wheel along the ground on our journies. Along the way, we must remember we are among others who are also on a journey of their own.

As the journey continues, so does the story.

The path you lead is yours to decide....

Now walk....

DO NOT BE AFRAID TO BE WRONG

I have painted the walls and ceiling and even the steps down into my basement studio. The step treads are purple, and the step risers are bright orange. I remember painting them at about six in the morning. My roommate came down on his way to work, and I looked up and said, "Genghis Khan was a great leader!"

Before I left for my trip to Florida, I painted part of the basement wall with phrases. The last one I painted read, "DO NOT BE AFRAID TO BE WRONG."

Walking up and down the stairs in a different state of mind now than when I painted that phrase, I interpret it with a new meaning. Before, I associated it with my artistic process. After being removed from the studio for three months without being able to create art, I now see it as a personal viewpoint on my own character as a human being.

Often times, we are afraid of taking chances due to what others will think or say. Perhaps out of fear or some other emotion, we are afraid to be wrong because, once we have done something wrong, we might feel as though we have failed ourselves or others. But we never know what an outcome will be if we do not try.

It is in trying that I am free.

DO IT ANYHOW

As I write this entry, I recline in bed. The temperature is near seventy degrees Fahrenheit, and there are clear skies with a slight breeze. The pain in my leg is near a level three, and with nerve spasms they reach a level four. I woke no less than four times last night, each time dripping from head to toe in sweat. I keep towels nearby to dry off with. My mind is depressed.

With laptop resting on my chest and my left leg propped up, I write on… There is no perfect situation in which to do anything, so do it anyway.

The perfect studio loaded with all the materials you could possibly want, the quiet room to write in, having no pain, no depression, and no unstable relationship, and so on. This is what makes great works of art, literature, music, and a balanced creative mind. It is all needed to produce something wonderful.

It is easy to fall, though. I did. And a large wheel ran right over my left leg. In the blink of an eye, I almost lost my life and left my family and friends. Almost. Any closer, and you would not be reading this material right now.

I surrender and let go and be patient with myself constantly! Yeah, the left foot hurts now. Yeah, my pride and ego and spirit have all been broken. But I must continue on. The truck that rolled over my body three and a half months ago still rolls down the road, and so do countless others who have suffered harship.

Why not I?

I can roll on, too. Sure, it will be a trial full of pitfalls and potholes along the way. But I am not alone if I choose not to be. I can ask for help if I choose to. I can call or knock on a neighbor's door. If I choose to.

I think back to a man who sometimes came to the rehab floor of the hospital. I forget his name. He had most of one leg missing and would fit prosthetics for the patients. He was one of the founders of extreme sports events for people with prosthetics. Standing next to him at six weeks in my walker, I got the idea that life just rolls right along. No excuses not to be doing that myself.

There is nothing but our minds to stop any of us from doing what we want. If I can write after all that has happened to me, if people are just rolling on no matter what.... Then surely you can do the same.

SPIRITS ARE ALL AROUND

Spirits have been in my life, carrying me through and helping me survive my drinking and drug use. Spirits were always with me in the studio. There were there that day I was sprawled out on the floor of my studio, which was covered with sheets of dry wall. My arms reaching out, my fingers moving small pieces of plaster around that had broken loose from the paper coating. Doom had seeped into my entire being. The spirits whispered, "Call your brother, who is sober. You cannot continue not drinking or using drugs without help. GET HELP!"

I reached for the phone that was kept on the floor and called my brother. I asked for help.

This started my journey into sobriety and a new life of love, joy and, most of all, freedom from the bondage of drinking and using drugs.

I am aware that spirits and angels surround me as I walk through life. We all are surrounded by them, even if we are not aware of them or even believe in their existence.

SPIRIT HOUSES

Spirits are all around us, whether you believe in them or not. A spirit house is an object that invites spirits in and shares their love with you.

I have made several spirit houses and have lead several spirit house making sessions. The results are beyond the creator's wildest dreams.

First, before you even touch the materials, you must be aware of what you want to bring into your world. It is best to use short statements. Love, Peace, Joy, Calm, etc. Once you have your idea in mind, focus on it and allow it to come into your world.

As an example, you can use a small cardboard or wooden bird house—they can be found at craft stores. You can use any small object, really, but the key component is to have a hole large enough to place small pieces of paper into your spirit house.

Continue to focus on your word or phrase—just let go and feel it. Now adorn your house with paint, collage, or anything you wish. Enjoy this time, and it is best to work in a group of other people who are creating spirit houses.

Once it is complete, write down small phrases that relate to your thought. Place these small pieces of paper through the hole of your house, and place the house somewhere that you feel it should be in your home.

Everyone who has made spirit houses, including myself, has had wonderful blessings bestowed upon them.

One woman, who had many horrible relationships with men, made a house for relationships. Within two weeks, she met someone and finally found a wonderful relationship.

Others have seen more joy and happiness come into their lives. I even made one for my art. Within a week or so, I got several phone calls and e-mails expressing interest in my art.

When the mind is clear and focused on what is wanted, the spirits listen.

RETURNING TO THE ART

I feel the spirits move me, and the art calls. The pain in my leg and nerve spasms continue in my foot, toes, and leg... The depression sharpens the pain....

Media calls.
Art calls.

I must go on....

How can I not return to the source after reading countless emails such as these?

I must endure the pain, depression, suffering, and all that I cannot bring forth out of my head and explain to you, the audience. I could take a lifetime of words and still never properly convey what it is...

The spirits are around, and I must go to the dusty studio—work through the black dogs and carry on!

Art healed me before. Art will heal me again. And art will continue to heal, no matter what happens to me....

Enough talk. To food, to studio, to art, to love....

Thank you for being with me on my journey. In peace and love, I hope to continue to hear, see, and talk to you along the remainder of my journey before I go back home to the light—till then, remember you are loved and protected.

.

ONE YEAR LATER

It has been one year since being run over by a tracker truck. Writing that sentence still rattles me to the very core. The whole event does not seem real and is even larger than life. I am not in denial that a semi-truck ran over me when I say it does not seem real. I was there. I saw the large amount of blood I lost, felt my bowels empty, and did not panic.... I died and faced the light. I then returned to live another day and to tell my story.

Since, then, many people have called me a living miracle, a hero, and one war-time veteran even said that he would surely have me in his foxhole with him.

A few questions were answered since the accident, and many questions surfaced. Why? What is the point of continuing on with life if I had done the full cycle? Beyond the daily physical pain and emotional trauma, somehow I must accept what has happened. My life is not the same nor will it ever be. I was there. Sometimes, I do not want to be here and want to be there.

When I speak of such things, my father scoffs and walks off. "The worst is over," he says.

But the worst is over for him. He does not wake drenched in sweat, snapping out of nightmares. He does not suffer other side effects of PTSD. When I speak of the other side or a new life, he just walks off complaining that I am talking about spirituality again. It is okay with me, though, that he and others think this way. How can they possibly understand? It is okay that they don't.

So, where do I go from here? I will do the next right thing. I will try to live in the moment. I will occasionally stray and think beyond the moment, which inevitably leads to a spiral of depression and negative thinking. So it is vital that I take care of myself. Eating and sleeping is important to my peace of mind and happiness. Creating art and being among other creative people is by far the greatest way to cope and learn about myself.

"Everything happens for a reason." We might question and debate that idea—I even questioned that very idea. But acceptance was the key that opened the door to a world waiting for me. Love is what I found. Love is all I have ever sought, and I found it…

Despite all the blood, pain, and terror, I would gladly do it all again. Without question, I would do it again.

Love has poured into my life. A love beyond measure of words or understanding has opened my eyes to a world beyond the lines at coffee houses, traffic, rude people, the repetitiveness of the everyday that people endure. These things I mention mean nothing to me. They are just there and are just what they are.

I was told for many years that I was admired, loved, and looked up to. It took being physically crushed to truly understand this love. The result often times raises a lump in my throat or brings tears to my eyes. Only now am I realizing, perhaps, that I died before I thought I had died.

This has been great to write about. It is a remarkable experience to be present during your death and to walk around today. Love is vital to my understanding to really feel emotion, be okay with that emotion, and move it through to the end. I learned it was OKAY to cry! And crying was something I did plenty of. It was a way to release pent up energy and to cleanse my wounds.

Anger is an emotion that is now lessening. That is not to say I do not show anger—it is now directed towards myself. Anger stems from my frustration and fear of situations. I have learned to step back and breathe and think, "Am I hungry? Am I tired? Am I feeling lonely?" Usually, tiredness and hunger are triggers. So I take nap or grab a healthful snack.

Love from others showed me that I am able to love myself. This took a long time to realize. I had the sense of being broken and damaged instead of being human. There is a lot of metal in me now, as well as the memory of a traumatic event. While showering and sitting on the toilet, I get to look at the physical scars that trigger conversations and images.

One psychologist told me, "Stop saying you feel 'broken.' You are broken." The walker I had been using gave that away.

And why is it that, when I used a wheel chair in public, it was a HUGE woman magnet! They would smile and go out of their ways to talk to me. Then I graduated from the wheel chair to the walker, which was a HUGE woman repellent! The walker made me become invisible, but at least I felt I could speak and act in a more dignified matter. That led nowhere, though.

I acted a bit. I went to the extreme, speaking and tilting my head. That was fun for a little while. The sideways glances made in public. The accents or 'play acting' I do in the retail store aisles do get a laugh and makes shopping almost tolerable through my painful limp. My phony accents include Southern, foreign accents, and rich and snotty. Now people are starting to request accents.

Bringing humor and silliness into my life and others' lives has become a way of coping with the horror I experience inside my head on a daily basis.

Sometimes, I hit a wall of depression that makes me numb and leaves me feeling as though I truly do not want to be alive. I wonder what the point is, and I think that all people strive to achieve is rather pointless.

The making of art has been consistent, though, and is the only thing that keeps me alive. Art is as vital as oxygen to me. Pure and simple acts of drawing or adding paint to a surface everyday has done far more for me than the three people I paid to listen to my problems.

The unhappy cry from others for material possessions is all around me. There are many people who I know personally that have excessive amounts of wealth but are still depressed.

One year later, the nights are often the same as those I spent in the hospitals. I wake several times with nightmares and sweats that leave me dripping wet. The only difference is that I now can walk to the bathroom, I am free from wires and tubes, and the screaming has stopped.

It is a burden too big to handle to explain how it really is from day to day when I am alone with myself. I do what I have to do, though, to get through.

Today, how do I cope? I take the day as it comes. If it gets too much, I retreat to my bedroom and watch a movie, read, or sleep. Usually, the extra sleep is a vital part of feeling better. Napping during the day may be the only way I can get any deep, peaceful sleep. People have often told me that by taking naps during the day, I am causing my lack of sleep at night. I tell them I sleep when I can, as monks say.

As I said before, sleeping and eating healthfully on a regular basis makes it easier to cope throughout the day. Then I can tell myself that at least I got up and cooked something. I look at everything I can manage after that as a blessing!

It all seems like a bad dream repeating over and over in my mind. The easy part was just lying back and following my instincts to stop the flow of blood. The hard part was and is what came next. Acceptance is the key. If I stop and think back to where I was a year ago at this time, then just being able to go to the bathroom on my own in the middle of the night is a blessing. Being able to feed myself is a blessing. The sole fact that I am alive is mind blowing and also a blessing!

Just a couple days ago, I was driving home from the grocery store, when a truck passed me. I stared at this truck and, as I do when I see any truck, I began to shake. Only this time, I realized it was the very same style of truck that had run over me.

The sheer length and and size of it made me cringe! To think that I was underneath all of that steel and rubber! Phew! It brought tears to my eyes, and all I could do was turn away and continue to shake.

Just a few minutes later, I was home again, went right to bed, and was just quiet. "I am alive. I am alive!" I kept repeating this, and the tears just streamed out of my eyes....

This is way too big for my head to grasp at times. Pulling every resource to get through the day is how I manage. I call friends, make art, write, watch a movie, or take a nap. I know that today might be my last, so I make the most of it.

I am an artist, and I must hold true to the vow I took to the arts. In sickness or in health, for richer or for poorer, till death do we part. I almost died by wanting to draw in my own pool of blood. I choose life before art, though. So I saved my life.

This journey has been one beyond my wildest dreams, and I am still here to do the work that I was meant to do. I know I am being taken care of by a power far greater than myself. When I die again and do not return to the living, I will be loved.

SURVIVING AMONG THE LIVING

Tears stained my face, and I shook with a fear that I hope no one living ever has to experience. "It's not fair," I said in my therapy session for PTSD. I repeated, "it's not fair" over and over and over. More tears poured down, and my nose filled with mucus.

It was then that I remembered the name of my suck tube that took away all the blood and gunk that came up. Gerry. I had named my suck tube Gerry. The tube's tip was a clear, hard plastic that was changed often when it became jammed with junk—mostly blood. What Gerry could not take out of me was the memories, the pain, the absolute horror of everything I have had to experience from that first moment of the accident until now.

Surviving is just as hard, if not even harder, as I expected. Why would it be harder? People in my family have told me the threat is 'over.' Maybe for them, the threat is over. They saw the tubes that ran in and out of my body. But they didn't feel the tubes. They watched the blood drain from my lungs into bags. But it wasn't their blood. They were there during the day and part of the night. But they didn't get fed through a tube or mess their beds or hear the screams—some of which were my own. They could go back to a hotel and take a shower, eat a meal, go to the toilet, and recline in bed. I am not resentful of those things. They had a way and means to escape and decompress from the situation, and I am thankful for that. But I didn't have that luxury, and I never will. It will always be there.

I feel alone, like no one else can even begin to relate with what happened to me and what I continue to go through on a daily basis.

How do I cope? How do I manage to go on with life? As a recovering addict and alcoholic, how do I live with post-traumatic stress disorder without a drink or a fix? Honestly, I have no idea, sometimes. I think of them on a daily basis.

I know morphine would be my drug of choice. What keeps me clean and sober, though? One word keeps it green for me, and that is 'consequences.' I have a progressive fatal disease that wants to see me dead. This is the main thing that I have to remember. If I pick up a drink or drug now, I would start back up right where I left off. This is something that is proven at every meeting of Alcoholics Anonymous I go to. Even with those consequences in mind, though, I still think of drinking. And that is insane thinking that I cannot follow through with.

Somehow, by sharing what works for me to cope with my accident helps me cope with it. The fact is that I keep what happened close to heart—it is my 'story,' and I own it. It is very real. No one else can know what is really going on in me, physically or mentally. Nor would I wish it on anyone.

Sleep has been disrupted in a big way. Night sweats continue, as do the nightmares and dreams that are stimulating enough to wake me and keep me up. From what I have read and heard from others with PTSD, sleep is a problem. Sleeping when we can seems to be an answer. Naps are wonderful. Often times, I hear I would sleep better if I did not nap during the day. I beg to differ, as do the others with PTSD I have spoken to.

Night seems to be a hard time for me. At night, I remember what happened after my family left from visiting hours. Screams of the dying echo in my head. By morning, there would be silence in the hospital—those people had died. I would see the priests come out from behind the curtain, consoling a family member and discussing funeral arrangements. I had even had several priests come and simply pray over me…. One and a half years later, thinking of that nearly brings me to tears. That memory just doesn't go away.

Laughter and humor are key factors to coping. This is also true with others I know with PTSD. Good comedians are a blessing, and the classics are worth their weight in gold. A good friend of mine was dying of cancer and asked me how I coped with pain. She was in severe pain and dying.

I told her to sit down with her husband and watch as many funny films as she could. A few days later, she was smiling a little more and thanked me for suggesting humor to help her cope with her pain.

I held her hand a day or so before she died. I told her she would be ok.... I kept repeating, "You will be ok." I knew where she was going. I had been there. She cried and held my hand as hard as she could and did not let go.... I miss her.

Another thing that has helped me cope is to say out loud that I had been run over by a truck. I made it real and did not cover it up or hide it. I bring what happened out into the open and shed light on what it really is.

Why do I do this? I do this so I can avoid sugarcoating a bad situation—so I do not disregard the severity of the accident. I tried lying to myself at first. I told myself that everything was FINE and OKAY. But all the while I wasn't! I was shaking and experiencing flashbacks to the accident. And I see RED everyday. Blood red.

How can I cope with that?! I cope by admitting what happened and keeping life very simple. It is the simple things that make me smile and laugh and remember where I am and that everything will be okay.

What happens when PTSD is so great that it completely takes over and coping skills do not help? What then?!

I manage the best I can and ride it out. It may take a few minutes, a day, or several days. Curling up in bed and crying might be the thing I need to do. It is okay to cry, so I do. And it sucks! PTSD sucks! It's not fair. It may get a little better, but it will never go away completely.

This is a particularly bad time for me with PTSD, too. I just do not give up though! Good grief! A very, very large truck ran over me....

Not one word comes to mind to express how I feel or what I am thinking. Too many pieces are missing, and the fact is that I may never know more about the accident, and its affect on me is something I have to accept in order to continue through life. Without warning, I will shake, cry, or feel something deeply that I cannot explain.

I continue creating art to the best of my abilities, and I read something everyday. At the suggestion of my therapist, I continue writing this book. I simply write things down that we have learned. This may help me to understand just a little—and this may help others, too.

Here is what I have learned:

After several months, I finally broke down and sobbed, saying it was not fair that I had come so close to death and can remember so much. I talked about how I could not handle survival—I just became overwhelmed. Nothing appears to be physically wrong with me. Except for my slight limp from pain, no one would ever know that I'd been so close to death. I owe so much to my therapist for pulling out the bloody mess inside my head and telling me that the images and feelings will lessen but never go away completely. I did not want to hear this, but I know I must somehow live with my trauma, or it will own me forever.

As night fell and the daylight gave way to darkness, so my mind fell into shadow. The faces and words were clear to me. I shifted between drawing, reading, and writing. I stayed awake, sometimes out of sheer fear. It got so bad one night that I was hearing voices and locked my bedroom door. Clean and sober, I had heard voices.

In the morning, I shared the incident with a good friend of mine, and he told me that it was a sign that I was reaching enlightenment and understanding. I did not quite understand.

Only a couple days later did I comprehend. And since that night, I have not had fear of hearing voices. Having reached enlightenment, I realize I have gained nothing. Monks say they have gained nothing as well.

I have been to a world where few go, and I long to return every day. I have survived something that has no words, so I am unable to communicate everything I feel and know.

Somewhere out there is another person who is in the same boat as I am. There is another person with the same fears, the same pain, the same heightened sense of reaction to situations.

The critical point of terror has passed. The tubes have long been out of my flesh. There are no more soiled bed linens to change. The routine needle pricks for blood tests are over. The screams have been silenced. Everyone who had been around me has either gone home or been buried. It is the images, the sounds, and the pain that lingers. The memory lingers.

Most vivid, perhaps, is the knowledge that I was not alone on that corner as I suffered in my own blood and waste. No, I was with some divine love that showed me that I was worth living a life among even all those strangers who did not help. Something great believed in me and never dropped me and continues to carry me now.

I am overwhelmed by a sense of warm love when I think that I was not meant to die. That I have a purpose in life. That I have merit. So much money and energy poured into and out of the nurses, doctors, EMTs, strangers, cleaning crew, volunteers, therapy dogs, family—and on and on and on. All I can ever do or say in reply is "thank you."

Thank you, thank you, THANK YOU!

Whatever we have been through, are going through, or will go through, it is what it is and nothing more. It is a series of moments strung together that leads to the present and prepares us for our futures. By staying in the moment and just dealing with it, anything is easy. ANYTHING!

Every morning, I draw three pages, write three pages, and read three pages. I follow this ritual by watching some comedy. The book I am reading is called *Floor Sample*, written by Julia Cameron. Years ago, someone gave me a copy of the *The Artist's Way*, which I read, wrote in, drew all over, and then passed on to another artist. Someone also gave me *Floor Sample,* which is about Julia's life, experiences, strength, and hope. She also knows that the secret to doing something is just doing it.

Just do the work. She wonders how anyone can have a screenplay written to completion in only six weeks. HOW?! Just write three pages a day—no more, no less. In six weeks, you will have enough for a screenplay.

One can apply this theory to any task. As I write, I am forty years old and have always wanted to play music. Julia started writing songs at forty-five—when she decided to just do it, the songs simply flowed out of her! All I have to do is make a decision and try.

Last night, I was interviewed by a newspaper reporter about my children's book, *The Red Heart Book*. The book was created as a small Xeroxed piece and handed to friends two days before I left for Florida. Three and half months later, I came home.

People who I had given the book to said they carried it in their pockets and would read it throughout the day. It gave them the sense that everything would be okay and that they were loved. They thought of me, and their troubles that day did not seem so bad. They encouraged me to publish the book. Many months passed, and I did nothing. The seed was planted, though—it just needed me to water it.

One day, the sun shone brightly, and I knew what had to be done. I needed to publish the book. So I bought a guidebook to children's book publishing. Included was a listing of publishers. As I scanned the pages, I learned two things. First, one of the publishers only signed a few new authors a year—if any at all—and every company specialized in only certain books. Second, these publishers only paid five to ten percent in royalties. So out of the vast majority of writers, only a few are selected, and those few are only paid a small amount for their work. Unless book sales are high, profits tend to be low.

Then I thought, "Why do I want to publish?" My dream was to share the book with as many people as possible and to make some money while I was at it.

More time went by, and I became discouraged and forgot about the project. I gave up.

But my friends did not give up on me—they wanted to see the book in print! One day I got a text message that read, "I want a few copies of your book!"

Excited at the chance to sell, I gathered some of the hand-drawn copies I had on my shelf. I put them in a bag and handed it to my friend. She thanked me, and that was that. I went home thinking, "Yeah, but where is the money!" I did not say anything to her about it.

A couple days later, I saw her again, and she said, "Here are the books I don't want, and I will keep the rest."

Again, I went home without money. I said to myself, "It is what it is. The money will come."

A few days later when I saw her again, she asked, "How much do you want for the books?"

I was in shock!

She said, "Name your price!"

She had taken five books, so I said, "Fifty dollars."

"Okay," she said.

A few more days passed before I saw her again, and she slipped a piece of paper into my hands and said thank you. I placed the check into my pocket without looking at it.

At home, I finally opened it and discovered it was written out for more than what I asked for! At that point, I knew I needed to publish my book somehow!

About a week later, I got a phone call from a friend, who said her daughter was a senior in high school and wanted to do an internship with me as a studio assistant. Here was the help I needed for my book! Yes! I was happy to have her help me in the studio!

The day she was to come, I was online and typed in a search for publishing. I had done this countless times before and had been led nowhere. This time, though, the very first site I found was called Create Space, a subsidiary company of Amazon. I liked what I saw.

When my studio assistant arrived, we sat down together, went through the website, and learned how easy it was to put a book up—a real printed book with a barcode and all the bells and whistles! We looked at each other, knowing we were going to put out what the public had wanted for so long! It took a few revisions of the book until it was ready for sale online.

Now, all people have to do is go to my website, click on the link, and order a copy. A printed copy will arrive by mail in only a few days.

After figuring out how I was going to publish *One Breath at a Time*, I had to work on promoting it. I did not give up because I could see how sharing my story would spread love! In fact, that is what got me thinking about how I could market it.

I called the newspaper that did the story on my accident, and they agreed to do a follow-up story about the book. A few days before the interview, I thought I should post a video of me reading the book on my website. I emailed the first video I shot to a few people, and they all said I should redo it. I agreed!

On the very day of my interview, I had to record another video. But I had no camera. I made a phone call to borrow one, and it was uploading just hours before the newspaper interview. Then some viruses that had infected my computer closed the browser, and my upload was lost!

I then only had one hour before the reporter would arrive. Where would I be able to upload my video in just a few minutes? I figured the library across the street had a super-fast connection, so I walked over there, connected to the internet, and in five minutes I had my video uploaded! After that, I altered my website to feature the video.

The reporter came, and, by following a page of written key points, we did the interview. I went to bed that night knowing I had gone the distance to get the job done!

I must preserve my memory of these moments so they stay as happy as they were when they occurred. When PTSD strikes, it is a struggle to remember all that was and is good. It is a struggle to roll with a flashback and remind myself that it will pass—it may not seem so, but it will. PTSD sucks! It really does.

For as long as I do not drink alcohol or use drugs, I have a chance to live. Sometimes, the PTSD gets bad, and I do want to use. But I cannot act upon those urges. Only hell and misery would result. And I do not want to return to that.

I just woke from a two-and-a-half-hour nap. Now, I'm reflecting on a stupendous weekend!

My hope today became a reality.

I'd had an idea that the show I was going to be in on Friday was going to be extremely well-attended. Furthermore, the show was only going to be 3 hours long, with sixty artists! How was I going to set myself apart from others and do my best?

I decided that my art that night would consist of small paintings and drawings that would be happy, fun, and accessible. I priced my art at a range of only twenty-five cents to forty-five dollars. Under my table, I had three large bins with overstock art. When something sold, I put up another piece of art right away. I had to because the wall was only just a little over four feet wide and nine feet high.

I turned my small space over three times, and I made more money in those three hours than at any other show I've been in. People were ecstatic, and so was I. It was possible to be set apart from sixty others, and I did it!

Now I want to find more ways to make my art so accessible to people while keeping it happy and fun! Everyone should be able to afford art in all forms if they want it. Art heals. Art brings a smile to one's face. Art is pure energy that keeps me and others alive and happy.

Depression still seeps in, though, and when it does I cannot afford for it to happen for long.

How do I ward off depression? First, I understand how it manifests when it first begins. I cannot become too hungry, angry, lonely, or tired. Taking care of those four things is critical to my wellbeing. If I am still depressed after that, I make sure that I am standing vertically so all the junk in my head will drain out. Music that is punchy and full of energy helps, too—as does wearing my studio clothes, sloshing paint around, and making art.

And if all that still fails, then I go for a walk or call someone and get into action just doing something. And there is always comedy! Especially the kind that makes you wet your pants, laugh till your sides hurt, and fall down, gagging and coughing. Laughter really is the best medicine.

The best way I can explain myself at this point is to say that I am not human. Before the accident, I had always felt like an outcast. After the accident, I knew I was not human and from another planet. I was not better than anyone else or smarter than them—I just wasn't human.

The only way I can cope and go on with this new life is to take it one breath at a time with a passion, love, and a kind heart while creating art.

I have been told that people who are cracked are blessed. They let the light in. I feel more broken than cracked, though, and I let in as much light as I can. It is in the light, art, and, life that I am truly free.

I have been where the fire burns all night.

I feel closure now and a little more at ease now that this book is done and put out into the universe.

Art heals....

NOEL

On Christmas Eve, 2011, I was told about a Pit Bull Terrier mix named Noel that was at the Delaware County SPCA.

I had been thinking of getting a dog for a while. Just the week before, my dad was telling me I should get a dog. The SPCA was closed on Christmas Day, so I went the following day with a completed application I got from their website.

www.delcospca.org

Noel was out in the yard being walked by a volunteer. Noel came right up to me, wagging her tail and licking me. It was magic.

Noel had been at the center for six weeks, having been brought in as a hit and run victim. The vet saved her life, however her right leg was badly damaged and had to be removed.

Noel and I had similar stories.

I was second in line for adopting Noel. I had to call back after 6 p.m. that same day. I did, and no one had called for her! They said I could come the next day at noon to pick her up! YIPPEE!

I could hardly eat, but I still had dinner! I was giddy!

The next day at noon, I was at the SPCA with the biggest smile! Noel was coming home with me!

I picked her up and placed her in the back seat on the bed I made for her… going home!

Within ten minutes at home, Noel was on the couch with me watching a movie, licking me, wagging her tail… so happy! We bonded and became buddies!

At 8:30 p.m., Noel got her first visitors of four woman bearing treats for her and a beautiful card welcoming her to the neighborhood. In the days following, Noel received many gifts of food, beds, rawhide bones, shampoo, and so much more!

I decided a part of my art sales would go to the SPCA that Noel came from. If you want to donate or buy art, please email me. Noel and I would love to hear from you!

Write to David and Noel at: davidgerbstadt@gmail.com

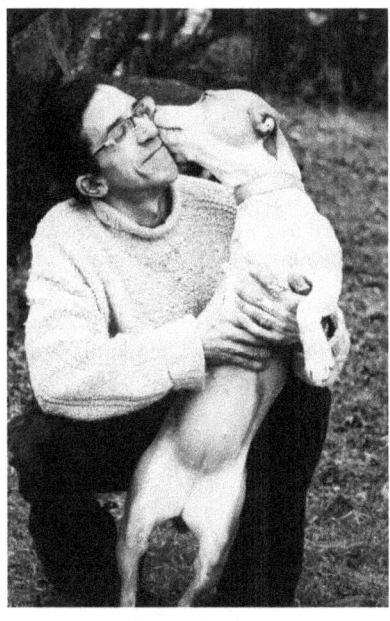

David and Noel
Photo by: Tony & Elaine Babcock
www.visualperceptions.biz

ABOUT THE AUTHOR

David Gerbstadt graduated from Millersville University in 1992. It was in college that an art instructor encouraged David to declare himself as an art major.

Without much prior influence, David dove into the world of art and never resurfaced.

David has shown his art all over the world and has collectors in the United States and over eleven countries.

From 1994-2002, David left for the taking over five thousand paintings and drawings done on found materials. "David was here," a documentary film about David leaving his art for the taking, was produced by three film students in 2002 and shown at the 2003 Iowa Documentary Film Festival, winning best audience pick.

After the release of the film, David no longer leaves his art for the taking. The film "David was Here" can be viewed online.

David is now a full-time artist, children's book author, and motivational speaker.

To contact David Gerbstadt
For art or for booking as a motivational speaker
e-mail: davidgerbstadt@gmail.com
Look for David on facebook

Books by David:

One Breath At a Time
Order online: amazon.com
search: One Breath At a Time David Gerbstadt

The Red Heart Book
Order online: amazon.com
search: The Red Heart Book David Gerbstadt

www.ingramcontent.com/pod-product-compliance
Lightning Source LLC
Chambersburg PA
CBHW070558100426
42744CB00006B/323